Where To Now?

THE ULTIMATE GUIDE TO YOUR

CAREER TRANSITION

FOR EXECUTIVES ON THE MOVE

Edua Potor

ISBN-10: 0987549804
ISBN-13: 978-0-9875498-0-8

Deposit number: DEP635023932228929390
Date: 24/04/2013 09:40:22
Locarno Code: 01-01
Deposit & Timestamping Service **www.Copyright-Australia.com**

Cover and Interior book design and formatting by Codruț Sebastian Făgăraș

For You,
THE AGELESS EXECUTIVE

TABLE OF CONTENT

Introduction to the Effective Career Management System

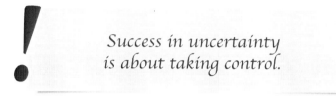

*Success in uncertainty
is about taking control.*

The aim of this book is to support executives and leaders during these competitive times. **ECMS** is a cost effective and easy to use step by step system, a suite of documents, and advice to build or rebuild, re-launch re-start-your career.

These are designed specifically to work with you, the external and internal leader to maintain control of your career and re-position yourself to leverage the opportunities of the next emerging cycle.

This is critical to get right, in times of uncertainty and dramatic change.

ECMS will quickly execute and integrate into your environment, and open new doors.

This competitive value proposition is unique in its completeness and simplicity and provides you with the best researched solutions available. In addition, methodologies, imparted in easy to follow modules in this book, will give you tools to yield results with high levels of satisfaction and effective outcomes.

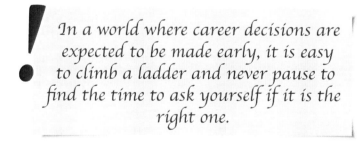

*In a world where career decisions are
expected to be made early, it is easy
to climb a ladder and never pause to
find the time to ask yourself if it is the
right one.*

Who you are is what you do. Is this true? Or are you performing under a false identity because this is what is expected of you, or because you thought that this was actually who you are?

Do you know yourself professionally and otherwise?

Do you know **what you want to do**? If you do, do you know **how to get there**?

Do you know **what you can do**? What you are capable of achieving?

These questions are the foundation of a successful career and successful career transition.

Many of us have "chosen" a position, because it was available at the time, and remained in a particular line of business within an industry in that fashion.

Most executives have pursued studies and acquired a degree in a discipline they wanted to specialise in and remained in that field for the rest of their career.

Yet, career decisions are not always made successfully so early in one's life or they may have been made led by circumstances which are no longer appropriate to your abilities or desires.

So, what happens if you wish to change direction? Or step up to the next level?

How do you handle change?

How do you review your career objectives and plan strategically to achieve your goal?

> *If you don't know where you want to go, you will probably end up somewhere else If you don't know where you're going, how will you know if you got there?*

This system will support you in clarifying for yourself what your next step should be.

It could be a step sideways in another industry; it could be a step up or a complete change.

What if you have been head-hunted and don't have an updated resume? You probably have not been subjected to an interview either. So how would you handle this scenario?

> *You may be the best candidate but if you don't know HOW to show it, How to communicate it, You may miss a life-time opportunity. Don't let a lack of "Know How" rob you of your rightful chance.*

Take the example of a respected Managing Director of a company in Europe. He poured all his resources, energies, knowledge and networks into a company that was not "supported" by the CEO and was undermined by additional ownership forces. However, with total commitment, regardless of the situation, he engaged himself in the pursuit of prosperity generation for the company. Indeed, the purpose of his role was to deliver profits. This he did, and this is to be commended, really, but ultimately, he forgot to put himself in the equation, at a cost to his health and relationships. He only re-assessed his career when his health was affected.

Diminished self-esteem and dissatisfaction are also common results of this driven attitude.

How often do we read about these situations? Or maybe you know someone just like this?

What happened to your dreams, your aspirations?

We all want to make a difference, to contribute to our company, to our life, to our loved ones.

The good news is that it is not unrealistic, with the right system.

> **!** *It is essential to regard yourself as a business.*
> *Businesses are built on a vision, then planning followed by action.*

So, the first rule is to begin with the end in mind and get into action.

The good news is that **ECMS** will enable you to get the first two components in place. All you have to do is follow the system and participate in the modules.

That is all!

ECMS, will guarantee the outcome you are searching for.

The thinking and the planning has been done for you. All you need to do is to enthusiastically participate in the system.

This system is dedicated to you!

To Your Success!

Edua Potor

Your Career Planning

Is it Time For a Change?

When is it a good time for a change?

Is it too late? Or too early? Or not quite the right time?

If you are reading this book, obviously you made the decision to change.

Up, down, side-ways, into or out-of a company.

As you know, any "controlled" change requires preparation.

This preparation will encompass you developing an effective marketing strategy, acquiring additional skills either in management or in attitude, definitely saving funds.

In the first unit, we will first cover your career vision and the plans required to bring your aspirations to fulfilment.

Get Elected to the Career of Your Dreams

Wasn't there excitement in the last American election! To think how President Obama emerged to become President of the United States! And he was re-elected!

Barack Obama was raised by a single mother. He was by no means wealthy, and did not necessarily have a lot of opportunity or resources to become President. However, he was able to build what is probably the most dynamic political campaign in history.

You too can climb up the ladder of success in your chosen career, with just two key factors:

Number 1: HAVE A VISION.
Knowing exactly what you want to accomplish is necessary if you want people to buy into your vision and support you in reaching your goals. Spell out your vision in a way that inspires and attracts people. A strong vision becomes magnetic. People are then attracted to what it is that you're trying to accomplish.

Number 2: COMMUNICATE with CLARITY, CONSISTENCY AND CONVICTION.
There are three dynamics to strong business communication: when you speak clearly you help people to further understand the purpose of your vision, and your path for getting there. The more you communicate with clarity, the more confident people are in your ability to lead.

Consistency in business communication is important because people want to know that you are genuine, that you are who you say you are and that you are going to do what you say you're going to do.

Communicate with conviction. The truth is that people will remember the level of passion with which you speak far more than the level of precision. Impressions are largely a product of demeanour and how you sound. Communicating with conviction is a strong business asset.

Just to recap, build and enhance your career by having vision and communicating with clarity, consistency, and conviction. By integrating these lessons into your daily life you can get yourself elected to the career of your dreams.

We'll concentrate on the written form first, with the **ECMS** system, so that so that you can use this information at meetings, networking events and interviews, with the conviction that will bring you the success you deserve.

So, let us now start this journey together.

Summary of the Career Planning Section

This section will cover the following:

- Present career choice
- Past career choices
- Patterns of recurring interests
- Talents/ abilities/ skills you have used in work and in life
- Talents/ abilities/ skills currently used
- Preferences
- Exploration of possible positions and data harvesting
- Relinquish what is not relevant
- How does this new potential reality stack up? Is it realistic?
- Career action steps
- Final Mission Statement for your life and your career
- Setting up goals
- Action steps
- Projected achievement dates

These components are addressed chronologically, to define what you want first, analyse what you have, follow the structure and lastly, a plan of action utilising the work already done.

Stepping into accomplishment.

Please note that we supply you with a system that has proven to work, but ultimately, success is connected to your acceptance of responsibility for your choices and actions.

We are unable to control the circumstance or foresee the consequences of any actions you may take. In choosing to proceed, you agree to accept the responsibility and benefits of this program.

It is your career, you are in charge!

About the Exercises

You may like to write onto these pages, or you may prefer to write on separate sheets of paper, and review and refine your comments further.

You may decide to concentrate on some of the exercises and not complete all of them.

This is fine, of course. Just remember that the effort, passion and commitment you put into these advices and instructions will directly reflect what you will get out of it.

> *You will find it quite valuable to reflect on your career situation, and ultimately the choice you will make for your new direction.*

Make a decision to use this book to give you the constant support to create change for yourself, change for the better, an opportunity to improve your life and your career.

This need not be a solitary endeavour, you might wish to do these exercises with someone who is addressing change as well.

You each should then have your own book and fill in the sections together and de-brief after each exercise. This "buddy" system would give you some feedback about the balance of your perceptions.

Your Present Situation

A journey always starts in the present, so we will begin with you outlining your current situation. Where are you at? Are you working in a fulfilling job with the best company? Or the chances are that if you have invested in this book, your reality might look different.

Please describe your present situation:

_____

_____

_____

_____

_____

Your Previous Positions

You will find it interesting to look into repetitions with you previous choices and to see patterns emerging.

This may be a revelation to you, and if these patterns are supportive to you, good and well, but if that is not the case, this new awareness will highlight areas perhaps worth avoiding.

With each career change, describe your motivation for the move. Were you promoted? Were you made redundant? Were you headhunted? Was it a good move? How was your decision made? Did those changes have an effect on your current situation?

Starting with your first job:

- What was the motivation behind this first job?
- Why?
- Was it a good choice?
- What are the effects today from that choice?

Career move:

- What was the decision behind this move?
- Why did you make that decision?
- Was it a good decision?
- What are the effects of that decision today?

Career move:

- What was the decision behind this move?
- Why did you make that decision?
- Was it a good decision?
- What were the effects of that decision today? (I think "what are" is preferable, but up to you).

Career move:

- What was the decision behind this move?
- Why did you make that decision?
- Was it a good decision?
- What are the effects of that decision today?

Career move:

- What was the decision behind this move?
- Why did you make that decision?
- Was it a good decision?
- What are the effects of that decision today?

Career move:

- What was the decision behind this move?
- Why did you make that decision?
- Was it a good decision?
- What are the effects of that decision today?

You may need to add more paper, if you had more than 6 positions.

Have you noticed a pattern?

You will find the next exercise quite interesting as well, in terms of putting a score to your level of fulfilment for each role.

Your level of fulfilment will be reflected by the company culture, your responsibilities, your colleagues, your boss, career advancement opportunities, company training, etc.

Most fulfilling would be (5) and least fulfilling would be (1).

This exercise in itself will be quite revealing with specific scoring for specific companies, or specific responsibilities.

You will end up with a graph which will show you ideally an upward move with some fluctuations, but overall quite revealing

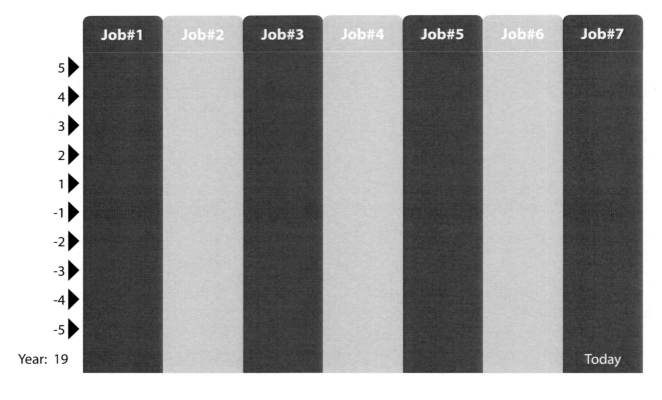

In the following table, list each position you've held and describe what you enjoyed and disliked about it:

	Position/Company	What I Enjoyed	What I Disliked

	Position/Company	What I Enjoyed	What I Disliked

What Do You Have to Offer?

Let's begin this section with an exercise developed by synthesizing the work skills predicted by leading Work Futurists to be important for future career buoyancy. Rate the following statements on a 3-point scale, as follows:

1. Doesn't describe me
2. Sometimes describes me
3. Always describes me

Statement	Rating
I do whatever it takes to get the job done	
I am willing to be measured on the results I create	
When making a decision, I prefer to act on the best information I have at the time, even if it is incomplete	
My customers' clients' exigencies generally demand that I solve the problem rather than delegate	
I have applied insights from a field other than my own in solving a problem.	
I have been instrumental in effecting a paradigm shift in some area of my work	
I have developed skills which enable me to tap into my intuition and perceptions	
I have expanded my skills for self knowledge and self observation during the past year	
I use feedback from others to improve my relationships with them	
My values and beliefs drive my behaviour	
It is easy for me to understand others without judgment	
I am skilled in conflict resolution behaviours	
I have sufficient practical business knowledge and skills to run a small business	

The next exercise is designed to detail your skills, i.e. what you do best. Skills fall into two categories.

1. **Technical skills**   relate to your particular area of expertise – the disciplines in which you are competent, such as computer programming, accounting or engineering.

2. **Transferable skills**   are the broad skills that can be transferred from one job to another or from one career to another. Your transferable skills have been acquired not only from your work, but also from your education, family and leisure activities. These skills are highly valued by employers.

Detail your **technical skills** below

_____

_____

_____

_____

_____

Rate the following **transferable skills** according to your perception of your competency, with a rating of 1 representing a low level of skill and 5 representing outstanding skill.

Transferable Skill	1	2	3	4	5
Implementing decisions, following through					
Exercising patience					
Creating egalitarian and accepting work environments					
Interviewing					
Listening					
Speaking one-to-one					
Public speaking					
Facilitating groups					
Writing, creative					
Writing, instructional					
Writing, persuasive					

Transferable Skill	1	2	3	4	5
Selling or promoting ideas					
Selling tangibles					
Motivating others to action; influencing ideas and attitudes					
Coordinating and managing people and projects					
Negotiating					
Reconciling and resolving; mediating					
Consulting; advising in an area of expertise					
Helping others to identify their problems, needs and solutions					
Facilitating personal growth and development of others					
Explaining complex concepts to others					
Lecturing; stimulating others to learn					
Enabling others to do their best work					
Observing people, data or things; awareness of details of these					
Remembering people, details, procedures, numbers, music, foreign languages etc					
Performing numerical, financial or statistical calculations					
Budgeting, forecasting, estimating					
Researching, investigating					
Analysing, defining constituent parts					
Evaluating ; diagnosing; judging people, information or things					
Solving problems					
Visualising concepts; seeing relationships, patterns, structure					
Translating others' ideas and concepts into a new form or situation					
Innovating, inventing, generating ideas					
Synthesising; integrating disparate parts into a cohesive whole					
Designing models of things; creating symbols					
Executing and carrying out decisions					
Planning; sequencing actions, tasks; arranging for functioning of a system					
Anticipating or predicting needs and problems					
Establishing priorities among competing requirements					
Achieving objectives; producing results					

Skills Analysis Summary

Now select the ten skills you see as your major strengths and prioritise them. Use examples where appropriate.

	1.	
	2.	
	3.	
	4.	
	5.	
	6.	
	7.	
	8.	
	9.	
	10.	

Remain Competitive

In the age of information, it is impossible to ignore change.

Some of you might remember a time when, in most companies, all documents were dictated to and typed by secretaries. They were the only ones who knew how to type. Well, just a few years later, EVERYONE has a PC, which means that EVERYONE KNOWS HOW TO TYPE and if they didn't, they had to learn quick smart.

You cannot rely only on your present skills. You must continuously develop new ones in order to remain competitive.

What skills must you develop today to stay competitive?

The definition of Job security is quite different to what it used to be. Not so long ago, you could rely on the company providing job security. Now the tables have turned and your career has to be driven by yourself.

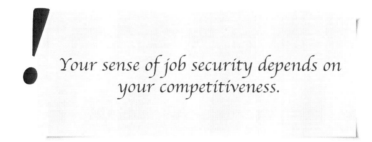

Your sense of job security depends on your competitiveness.

No longer does a company provide a position, with a well-defined position description and their expectations to find the perfect robot to fit in that "space".

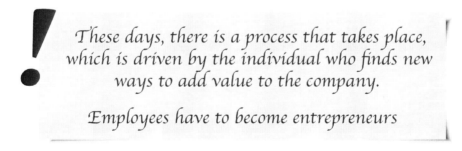

These days, there is a process that takes place, which is driven by the individual who finds new ways to add value to the company.

Employees have to become entrepreneurs

As mentioned in the early pages, employees have to see themselves as a small business unit.

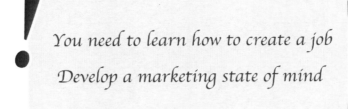

You need to learn how to create a job

Develop a marketing state of mind

If you create the habit of continuously learning, you always will remain marketable.

Whether an employee or self- employed, your success will be based on remaining marketable, on continuously learning.

Look back at what you have learned over the years, and who you have become as a result of that learning. How could all this benefit a client/customer/employer?

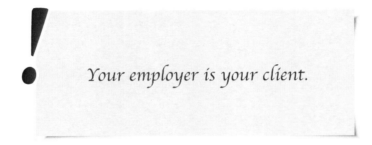

Your employer is your client.

Whilst employers are interested in what you can do, in general, they are mostly interested in what you can do for them specifically. You will be selling your expertise to them and what value will you be adding to them/their company? What is your special expertise?

Boost Your Career by Developing Your Personal USP

(Unique Selling Proposition)

ActionCOACH, the world's number one business coaching firm, teaches its clients to create and use a company or personal USP -- Unique Selling Proposition -- to gain traction in the marketplace and separation from competition. A good USP can also boost a career by helping employees define or redefine themselves in terms of the benefits they can offer a company and its bottom-line.

"With all the layoffs and downsizing, it is more important than ever to take an inventory of your skills, knowledge and abilities and create an identity that makes you the 'go to' person in your field."

What are the components of a good personal USP?

You need to make a statement that is:

- Benefits-oriented
- Something truly unique that no one else can offer
- Compelling enough to influence or motivate others to adopt the proposition

Superman's USP is a good example: "Faster than a speeding bullet, more powerful than a locomotive, able to leap tall buildings with a single bound"

This little exercise will help you find what your special value is, what your special expertise is. What do you do? What makes it unique?

_____

_____

_____

_____

Now, who needs your services? Who needs your talents? Any new target markets?

_____

_____

_____

_____

How would companies benefit from what you do?

_____

_____

_____

_____

_____

Do you see any new emerging developments in your target market?

_____

_____

_____

_____

_____

How would you present yourself as a solution to a company's problems?

_____

_____

_____

_____

_____

Why should YOU be the one delivering your talents in your chosen position?

_____

_____

_____

_____

What will you do this year to become more valuable in the market place?

_____

_____

_____

_____

What Do You Want in Your Career?

Most of you choices will be based on the values that you hold.

If you are a young parent, your values will revolve around your family and stability is most important. When stability meant remaining in the same company for 20 years, the decisions were easier to make, but at a price. Indeed - instead of the traditional 40 hour work week, salaried employees found themselves working more hours and taking work home too.

The new generation of workers is rebelling against this and wants a balance of life and work AND in that order.

Research has shown that some will take a lower salary in order to have that balance. The new generation wants their careers to match their values. Do you know what your values are?

Identify Your CORE VALUES:

Your work environment can be chosen for its ability to meet your needs. You must identify the work environment which will enable you to succeed and make your greatest contribution to the company.

Identifying your values provides purpose and direction to your career. The following list describes principles that people use to measure their level of satisfaction from their job. Assess each of these criterions and rate the degree of importance that you would assign to each for yourself.

We suggest the following scale:

3. Very important to me
2. Less important
1. Not important or even undesirable

Value	Rating
Having a stable and relatively unchanging work routine and job duties	
Having work which requires me to take risks and rise to challenges frequently	
Working in areas which would best utilize my talents	
Working in a company which is considered a leader	
Solving challenging problems and avoiding continual routine	
Being able to continually learn new skills and acquire new knowledge	
Being able to change and influence others' attitudes, opinions or behaviours	
Being directly responsible for work which is done and produced by others under my supervision	
Being recognized as associated with a particular organization	
Being able to depend on keeping my job and making enough money	
Working in a consistently ordered environment where has its place and things are not changed often	
Having day to day contact and dealing with the public	
Providing a service to and assisting others as individuals or as groups	
Developing close friendships with co-workers and customers	
Working mostly in a team	
Working mostly by myself on projects or tasks	
Having work which can lead to substantial earnings or profit compared to the norm	
Receiving public recognition for my work	

Value	Rating
Having opportunity to work hard and move ahead in my organisation	
Having responsibility and accountability for determining outcomes for myself and others	
Being able to direct and control the course of my work	
Being responsible for the planning and implementation of tasks and projects as well as for the people involved	
Being able to integrate my working life with my personal life	
Avoiding pressures and the rat race	
Pitting my abilities against those of others in situations which test my competencies and in which there are win or lose outcomes	
Working in a job in which I can get involved in community affairs	
Making a contribution for the betterment of the world I live in	
Being respected for my position and title; having symbols of success	
Being free to plan and manage by own time schedule; having flexibility	
Building in-depth knowledge; being consulted by others and respected for my contribution to my profession	
Producing tangibles; things which I can see and touch	
Doing work that is novel and different from others' work	
Having opportunity to express my ideas, reactions, and observations about my job and how I might improve it	
Being involved in creative works of art; music, literature, drama etc	
Working in a place which is pleasing to me aesthetically	
Doing work that requires manual dexterity, physical demands, coordination	

Choose the top 5 values from those you have rated "3"

_____

_____

_____

_____

_____

What is preventing you from meeting all of your top 5 values?

_____

_____

_____

_____

_____

What changes do you need to make to meet these values and work towards achieving career satisfaction?

_____

_____

_____

_____

_____

Create the Life You Want by Finding Your Purpose

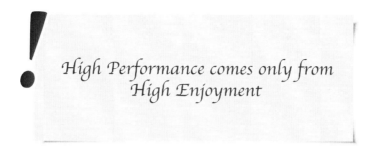

High Performance comes only from High Enjoyment

Your work may never satisfy all your personal needs. Trying to have your needs met from your work could cause you to neglect other areas of your life.

You will find some balance when you seek meaning in your work, whilst building skills and acquire experiences that are marketable.

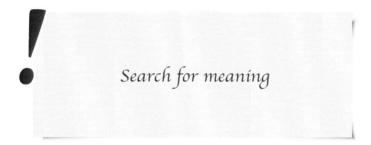

Search for meaning

Meaning is the ideal foundation upon which to build your career. Obviously, not all jobs will have the level of meaning you seek, but you will find that by putting your attention to it, you will get some insights that will guide you in the right direction with your decisions.

What is the most satisfying job that you could imagine or invent for yourself?

_____

_____

_____

_____

_____

What are your natural talents?

_____

_____

_____

_____

_____

What do you do really well?

_____

_____

_____

_____

_____

List activities you enjoy so much that you can lose yourself in them happily

_____

_____

_____

_____

How to Create a Balanced Life

Consider the circles below, as a representation of the total amount of time available to you.

Divide the **first circle** into portions representing how much time you spend in each of your activities.

Your present allocation of time:

With the **second circle**, go through the same exercise, considering how much time you would like to spend in each activity.

Your preferred allocation of time:

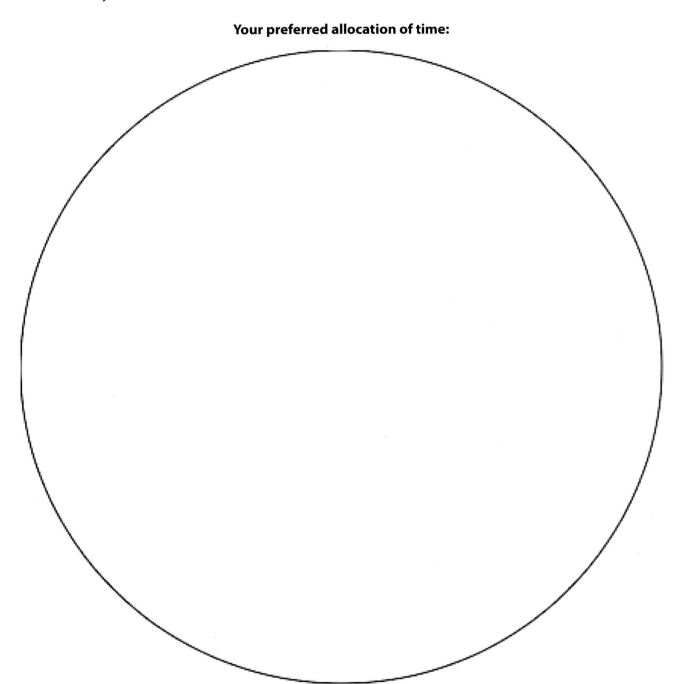

Activities in addition of your work would include: Family, social, spiritual, sports, leisure, hobbies, community, domestic activities, personal grooming, sleep, etc.

You will most probably notice a discrepancy between the first and second circle.

Which actions can you take to create more balance and satisfaction in your life?

_____

_____

_____

_____

_____

Create Your Personal Mission Statement

Try to summarize your vision using a powerful phrase in the first paragraph of your mission/vision statement. Capturing the essence of your vision using a simple memorable phrase can greatly enhance the effectiveness of your statement. This phrase will serve as a trigger to the rest of the mission/vision in your mind and the mind of those who read it.

This can take some time, but the most important thing is start working on it. And then come back to it later to refine it further, until you are completely satisfied with it.

This is your purpose/value/mission/vision business card

TIPS:

- Describe Your Vision Statement in the Present Tense
- Make your Vision Statement Emotional
- Add Sensory Details to Your Vision Statement

Short Term and Long Term Choices

Texas oil billionaire H.L. Hunt once said that there are only two ingredients necessary for success. The first is that you have to decide exactly what it is that you want.

This is where he believed many stumble. They never decide what it is that they really want.

They may think they want something from time to time, usually something generic and vague like "being rich" or "a better job," but it's just a fleeting thought; they are never truly clear on what these things really mean.

Hunt said that once you've decided what it is that you want, the second ingredient is to determine the price you have to pay to get what you want, and then resolve to pay that price by establishing your priorities and getting to work.

We will enter into the goal setting section later in the book, but right now, this concept is an introduction to long term and short term desires you have for the industry or profession you most like to work in. The reason for Short and Long term differentiation is that there is a period of transition between where you are and where you want to be. This process clarifies the various salient points that need to be considered.

Short term desires

_____

_____

Long term desires

_____

_____

What are the characteristics of this role?

Short term

_____

_____

Long term

_____

_____

What kind of salary do you need? Want?

Short term

_____

_____

Long term

_____

_____

Who would be your ideal boss?

Short term

_____

Long term

_____

How would your boss' attributes affect you?

Short term

_____

Long term

_____

What are your top 5 career choices/ roles?

Short term

_____

_____

_____

Long term

_____

_____

_____

Concerns and Solutions about Your 5 Choices

Concerns: _____

_____

Solutions/Actions _____

_____

Concerns: _____

_____

Solutions/Actions _____

_____

Concerns: _____

_____

Solutions/Actions _____

_____

Concerns: _____

_____

Solutions/Actions _____

_____

Concerns: _____

_____

Solutions/Actions _____

_____

Generating and Choosing Alternatives

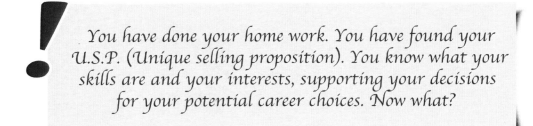

You have done your home work. You have found your U.S.P. (Unique selling proposition). You know what your skills are and your interests, supporting your decisions for your potential career choices. Now what?

This is the time when you need to take an active role in decision making about your career.

Your commitment does not require the assumption that there is only one position in the world that is right for you at this stage. There is still some latitude available to you, but you need to be clear about your skills and interests and also be flexible about how and where you will apply them.

Exercise:

List your possible role, position title or career choices. Then rate each on a scale of 1 to 10 for each of the factors listed, using the following definition:

- **Satisfaction:** Does this choice excite you? How do you **feel** about it? Would it fit your passion?

- **Realistic marketability:** Do you have the skill base to realistically pursue this option? Are you willing to take the steps required to make the transition if you don't have the skills now?

- **Potential for achieving life and career goals:** How does this choice fit, based on the answers you gave to the section "Creating a Balanced Life?"

- **Industry outlook:** What are the global workplace trends, market trends, demands and opportunities in this area?

Role / Job Title / Career Choice	Satisfaction	Realistic Market-ability	Potential for Achieving Life and Career Goals	Industry Outlook	Total

This exercise should provide you with solid clues to the career objectives that will be most appropriate for you.

In addition to your self-assessment, there are other sources of information about a particular position or industry.

!
The best source of information about a particular position or an industry is the people working in it.

Some further source of information for your career:

- Published information is a good source
- Interview people who work at the roles your are considering
- Go to seminars
- Get involved with professional groups
- Learn how to network effectively - This is covered further in this book starting on Page 137

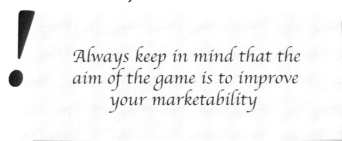

!
Always keep in mind that the aim of the game is to improve your marketability

Compose Your Career Objective

An employer will be looking for you to express your career aspirations. Your career objective may be stated in your cover letter or it could head up your resume document. Use it as an effective marketing statement, tailored to your career goals.

It tells the employer exactly what you want and shows that you have direction. If your previous roles are different from the direction you are now seeking, or in a different/ allied industry, then an objective communicates your decision to change careers.

Here are a few examples:

- A chief Executive or senior management role with the opportunity to achieve outcomes using my strategic management, communication and problem solving skills.
- Innovative fundraising professional for various nonprofits and universities. Meets and exceeds campaign goals through consistent donor relationship development, incremental giving strategies and decisive planning with campaign and agency directors. Seeking to manage an advancement team focused on growth potential and cultivation of relationships.
- A safety management role in an organisation committed to a systematic design approach to safety implementation
- A senior line management or information officer role with overall responsibility for improving the fulfilment of strategic business information requirements in a substantial organisation.

Draft your career objective, both in the short term and in the long term:

Short term
_____

_____

Long term
_____

_____

CONGRATULATIONS!

You have completed your career planning section! You have drafted your career objectives and now, let's move to the action part of the **ECMS** system.

Your Career Strategy

Your Career Goals

One of the toughest issues in making a good career choice and career goal setting is reaching clarity.

Most people, even very successful ones, have some periods in their career path when they seem unsure about their career choice and goals, or when their career is "halted", they need external impetus to know how to take the next step.

The following table provides you with a simple outline of the factors you may want to consider and identify when setting and analysing your career goals in a step by step format.

Career Goal You must define and write them down in order of priority	Benefits and Advantages of achieving this goal listing these may help to motivate you	Key Steps That you need to take	When Will I do This? Give yourself deadlines	Support and Resources (What support and from whom do I need, what resources, such as time, money, contacts)	Outcomes and Reflection (Record whether you achieved the goal and what worked or did not work along the way for future reference)

These questions will be addressed in the goal setting system and when answered, you can then prioritise them.

Who	What	Where	When	How
Who will I ask for help?	What do I want the outcome to be?	Where should I start?	When should I begin?	How should I begin?
Who will benefit from my career goal?	What will I do to get started?	Where will my career goal put me in 6 months, 3 years?	When Do I want these goals to be reached? Short term, long term goals.	How will these goals affect my future?
Who will I work with to accomplish my goal?	What will really satisfy me?	Where will I apply my resources?	When will I apply my knowledge to begin attaining my goals?	How do I really feel about the goals that I have chosen?

For example, if you are a National Manager and want to move up to a General Manager within your company; or if you need to move "out" to another company, to achieve this goal, you will need to put these steps into place;

		Steps for How	Steps for answering what	Steps for why	Steps for When	Steps for where
	1	I will make a to-do list	I will put my ideas for company improvement in it	I want to move up the next executive position	I will do this today! I will do this on the week-end.	I will do this in private
	2	How can I get noticed by the CEO?	I will make a presentation showing my idea for improvement within the company	Because I can't move up if the CEO does not know of my capabilities	I will do this the day it is finished	I will do this at work
	3	How can I let my work be seen	I will now show presentation to the CEO	I know my work is good and strong	I will do this when I know the CEO can't ignore me	I will do this in the CEO's office.
	4	If my goal is to move out and enter a new company to speed up the "promotion" How can I get noticed by head hunters? How can CEO's of other companies see my work?	I will schedule time with a major company player to give my ideas	I can't move up until I acquaint myself of the right players	I will arrange a meeting with a head hunter or a CEO this week.	I will do this during a meeting on their premises.

Four strategies can help you to develop an effective action plan.

- **State your goal in very specific terms that you can accept**
  Set goals over which you have as much control as possible, where your performance is the goal, not the outcome. The outcome will take care of itself anyway, maybe in a different way or time than what you anticipated.

- **Set Goals that stretch you**
  You should set goals so that they are slightly out of your immediate grasp, but not so far that there is no hope of achieving them.

- **Plan backwards from your goal for the best results**
  If you set out to achieve a goal in 3 months, what do you need to do today? Next week? Diarise it; put it in your electronic diary at work, as a reminder, or in your blackberry.

- **Confront your fears and expectations immediately and progressively**
  What are the possible risks, or obstacles? What are possible solutions?

- **Put your plan on paper and into action as soon as possible**

- **Achieving your Goals**
  When you have achieved a goal, you have to take the time to enjoy the satisfaction of having done so. Absorb the implications of the goal achievement, and observe the progress you have made towards other goals. **Reward yourself!**

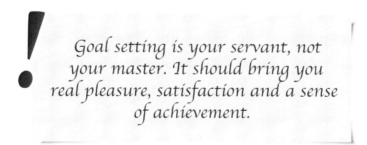

Goal setting is your servant, not your master. It should bring you real pleasure, satisfaction and a sense of achievement.

The following exercise will help you concrete your action plans, based on a 3 year plan.

You can choose the first written format, or the table following it, to provide you with an instant visual overview.

Goal in 3 Years

_____

_____

Why I want to achieve this goal

_____

_____

Any Risks/ Obstacles?

_____

_____

Possible Solutions

_____

_____

Goal in 1 Year

What do I need to achieve, in one year, in order to be in line for my 3 year goal?

_____

_____

Why I want to achieve this goal

_____

_____

Any Risks/ Obstacles?

_____

_____

Possible Solutions

_____

_____

Goal in 6 Months

What do I need to achieve, in one year, in order to be in line for my 1 year goal?

_____

_____

Why I want to achieve this goal

_____

_____

Any Risks/ Obstacles?

_____

_____

Possible Solutions

_____

_____

Goal in 3 Months

What do I need to achieve, in 3 months, in order to be in line for my 6 months goal?

_____

_____

Why I want to achieve this goal

_____

_____

Any Risks/ Obstacles?

_____

_____

Possible Solutions

_____

_____

Goal in 1 Month

What do I need to achieve, in 1 month, in order to be in line for my 3 months goal?

_____

_____

Why I want to achieve this goal

_____

_____

Any Risks/ Obstacles?

_____

_____

Possible Solutions

_____

_____

Goal this Week

What do I need to achieve, this week, in order to be in line for my 1 month goal?

_____

_____

Why I want to achieve this goal

_____

_____

Any Risks/ Obstacles?

_____

_____

Possible Solutions

_____

_____

Possible Goal	Short Term	Medium Term	Long Term
Initially, working only 5 days, as a general rule	X		
To move into a senior sales management role with a multinational company		X	
To complete MBA			X

Review Your Career Objectives

Has the previous exercise caused you to want to re-assess your objectives, or have they remained the same as set out in the first module of the book, or do you wish to refine them?

Short Term Career Objective:

_____

_____

Long Term Career Objective

_____

_____

Keep Focused and Keep Motivated

Positive goals that are geared toward your pleasure are much more powerful motivators than negative ones that are based on fear. The right combination of both is the most powerful and motivating mix.

Here are a few ways for you to remain motivated:

- Visualise your future success and reproduce the feelings you'll experience when you achieve it
- Mentally walk the path towards this success, set milestones along the way, feel the feelings you would have at each milestone.
- Assign a high priority to each task that you must achieve which will give each task a priority in your mind
- Set a target for the amount of work you will do each day, each week, toward your goals
- Create a picture of what the desired outcome will look like, and have this vision in your mind at all times
- Use visual indicators to monitor progress and complete the task
- Give yourself affirmations to remind yourself of how capable you are at reaching your goals
- Watch movies that motivate you or listen to music that motivates you
- Get help and support from people around you or from a professional in the field for example a personal trainer, a career coach, etc.
- Define your own version of success. Don't let others define success for you
- Focus on the positive achievements and not the negatives
- Share your successes with others

Your Goals Must Be Measurable

A measurable goal is structured as an affirmation statement. An affirmation statement allows you to visualise and bring to life the details of your goals. Its parameters include the answers to the questions What, Where, When, Why and How.

Here are a couple of examples of measurable goals and note the use of present tense and positive language.

- By December of (year) I am earning $...........as my total annual remuneration package. I am achieving exceptional results in highly competitive environment, as a results driven leader.
- In December of (year), I am living in a beautiful beachfront home, valued at $ .... or more, and I own it free of encumbrances.
- The above examples are monetary attributes. Can you add another measure – of quality of relationship, of physical and emotional balance in one's life? Would this also be the time to include the spiritual wellbeing?

Your Goals Must Be in Writing

How many times have you forgotten to do something because you did not write it down?

Statistics reveal that 3% of the people in the world have goals that are written down; the other 97% does not.

Perhaps the most revealing exposition on the importance of goals comes from a Harvard study. A synopsis of the study that was conducted at Harvard Business School between 1979 and 1989 is presented below. In 1979 the graduates of the MBA program at Harvard were asked a simple question: "Have you set clear, written goals for your future and made plans to accomplish them?" The results were very interesting. 84% had no specific goals at all, 13% had goals but they were not committed to paper, and only 3% had clear goals and plans that were written down. In 1989, a good ten years after the first phase of the study, the interviewers again interviewed the graduates of that class. Their results were even more startling. The 13% that had goals but not written down were earning twice as much as the 84% that did not have any goals. An even more interesting statistic is that the 3% who had written down plans and goals were earning on average ten times more than the other 97%. Furthermore the mere act of writing a goal down on paper increased its chances of being accomplished by a staggering 90%. Fantastic!

Writing Your Goal

Each of your long term goal will have a short term goal. Write them down starting with your long term ultimate goal.

Goal:

_____

_____

Goal:

_____

_____

Goal:

_____

_____

Goal:

_____

_____

If You Have the Commitment, the Drive and Determination to Achieve, You Already Have Half of What It Takes To Succeed!

Your Support Team

Remember to enrol a support team to see you through your journey

- Your loved ones: Your spouse or partner, your children, your parents, some of your friends. They will be your best supporters and will enjoy celebrating your successes along the way.
- Mentors in the industry; when you tell them of your aspirations, they will take an interest and even arrange introductions
- Executive Recruiters / Head Hunters
- Career advisors
- Career coach

List the significant people who will be part of your support team:

_____

_____

CONGRATULATIONS

- We have covered a lot of ground and addressed the following:
- The importance in having a vision
- How to communicate it
- The necessity of remaining competitive
- Developing your USP (Unique selling Proposition)
- Looking at your values
- Articulating your purpose
- Creating your career Objectives
- Stating you Personal Mission Statement
- Establishing your Career Goals
- Writing your goals
- Keeping motivated
- Getting your support team together
- Celebrating!

You will find the following table helpful as a one page record of your goals as they stand from today.

Goals at a glance

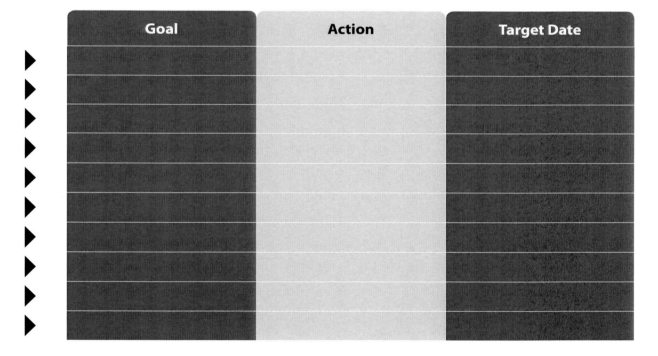

Goal	Action	Target Date

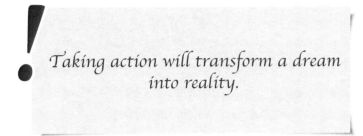

Taking action will transform a dream into reality.

This transformation will occur, even when initially there maybe uncertainty of success.

Whatever the demands of the move you are planning; its success will ultimately be largely determined by your attitude toward the project, and your execution of it.

We consider it a privilege to assist you in your journey and know that getting into action with your project will guarantee success.

Knowing what you want from a job is critical in your job search, saving you time and giving you an edge during interviews. Understanding this important part of your career profile will allow you to "sell" yourself to employers as the right person for the right job.

You sell yourself first in writing, through your resume, secondly through a face to face Interview.

We will address the resume compilation in the next section, of **ECMS** which is your next step in this career creation process.

It is critical to present a brand and value proposition-driven resume.

Your Resume

The Purpose of Your Resume

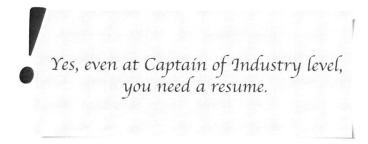

Yes, even at Captain of Industry level, you need a resume.

It is your written presentation document, which Executive Recruiters/Head Hunters, will need, prior to a meeting - even when there was a personal referral or prior relationship.

You definitely want Head Hunters, or potential employers to "get" you! And they need to have access to information that is congruent, on-brand, and consistent with the value messages you will be delivering in your resume and utilise in your interviews.

The first steps to lay the foundation for a solid resume, have been covered in the previous modules, where you worked through your likes/dislikes, your technical skills, your transferable skills, and summarised them.

You also drafted your career objective and listed your U.S.P. and assessed your values.

The next step is to put all this information together and complete your resume aiming to achieve the greatest clarity and what you are really offering to a company/ employer.

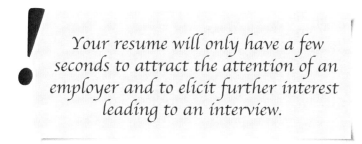

Your resume will only have a few seconds to attract the attention of an employer and to elicit further interest leading to an interview.

Take time to think about your accomplishments and how they have benefited your past employers. Ensure that you emphasize accomplishments rather than listing responsibilities.

Your unique contributions are the most critical information on your resume to executive recruiters and hiring authorities.

Of course, they want to know how many people you led or the size P&L you managed. It's important to provide the context of your positions. But keep that information brief.

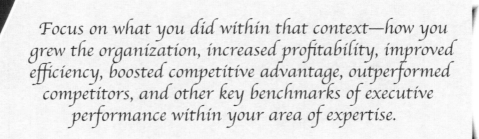

Focus on what you did within that context—how you grew the organization, increased profitability, improved efficiency, boosted competitive advantage, outperformed competitors, and other key benchmarks of executive performance within your area of expertise.

How to Write a Killer Resume

First and foremost, to be effective, your resume must

- Target a specific job and grab the reader's attention with strong selling points on why your skills and background "fit" the position you are seeking.
- Or, target a specific organization to create your own employment opportunity.

Either way, your resume needs to fit a position requirement or a company requirement.

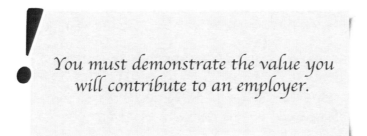

You must demonstrate the value you will contribute to an employer.

The Employer's Point of View

Potential employers are looking for people who have clear ideas about themselves and what they do best.

Employers want to know

- What value will you bring to the company?
- What specifically makes up this value?
- You need to substantiate that you have provided value in the past that is consistent with the value you will provide your new employer in the future.

Employers look for convincing evidence that candidates have the skills their vacancy or upcoming position requires.

Employers are most interested to find out

- What you can do for them?
- Do you meet their needs?
- Are you convincing in conveying your positive working attitude? Your drive?
- Have you expressed what a good fit you will be within their company's culture?

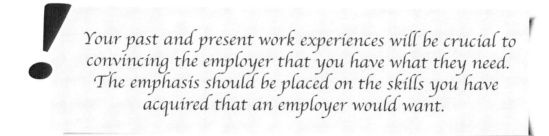

Your past and present work experiences will be crucial to convincing the employer that you have what they need. The emphasis should be placed on the skills you have acquired that an employer would want.

Employers regard your resume and cover letter as an indication of your performance, work ethics and your willingness to succeed.

Crafting Your Resume

The quickest way to catch the readers' eye and make them want to hear more is to show that you can produce value. Your most relevant skills, achievements, education and experience illustrate this value.

Remember that employers use resumes in several ways to:

- eliminate unsuitable candidates
- match your qualifications to their needs
- develop interview questions
- judge your communication skills
- guide the interview process
- remind them of you when hiring decisions are made
- compare you to other candidates
- justify their decision.

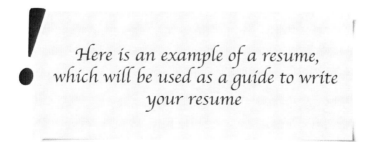

Here is an example of a resume, which will be used as a guide to write your resume

John D. Smith
27 Pacific Avenue
SYDNEY NSW 2000 Australia

Email: johndsmith@email.com.au
Phone: (61+2) 123 1234
Mobile 0411 213 123

CEO — CFO — GENERAL MANAGER

Strategic and hands-on executive, highly skilled in creating and executing blueprints for business growth. Consistent career record of achieving profitability, cost control, and operational improvement in highly challenging environments. Talent for building teams and instilling customer focus. Extensive international experience (multilingual, multicultural). Proactive and nimble in fast-paced, rapidly changing environments.

- Strategic Planning & Tactical Execution
- Multi-Site Operations Management
- Financial Planning & Analysis
- Accounting & MIS System Implementation

- P&L Management
- Staff Training, growth, Advancement
- Cost Control & Profit Enhancement
- Customer Relationship Management

EXPERIENCE AND ACHIEVEMENTS

Kent Food Group   2004–2008
Cremont, Ohio, USA ($50MM food-service provider to offshore and land-based facilities)
President and CEO
Revitalized the company. Stepping into interim "rescue" assignment, preserved key contracts, improved financial and operational performance, increased customer satisfaction, and created strategic and tactical blueprints for continued success and growth of the company.

- Gained 2 major accounts - 27% of total sales volume - by boosting visibility, customer contact, and customer service.
- Reduced food costs 3% and administrative labour expenses 4.5% by introducing accurate expense-monitoring systems.
- Increased client satisfaction level from 65% to 92%.

- Turned around organization, reengineered the internal-controls structure, created a smooth-functioning division supporting 21 clients in 123 locations.
- Enhanced training, communication, staff selection and performance.

EARLY CAREER

Managing Director, CountFast Accounting Services, Sydney, Australia   1987–1991
Launched and managed accounting practice serving medium and small businesses.
Grew business to 120 clients and negotiated its profitable sale.
Assistant Controller/Credit Manager, Acme Supplies, Sydney, Australia   1984–1987
Improved performance of the financial organization—reduced reporting times, shrank delinquent accounts, and cut costs. Drove conversion from manual to computerized accounting, invoicing, and inventory-control systems.
Senior Audit Manager, Oliver and Associates, CPA Firm, Sydney Australia,   1980–1983
Managed audits for manufacturing and industrial clients of this representative for Deloitte Touche Tohmatsu

PROFESSIONAL PROFILE

Education:	BAcc graduate	1984 — U.T.S. University - Sydney
Technology:	Real World Accounting	IBM System 34
	Peachtree Complete Accounting	AS/400
	Lotus 1-2-3	Hyperion
	MS Office	JD Edwards
Additional:	Global citizen and travel veteran through South and Central America, Europe and Australia
	Fluent Spanish, Brazilian and French; conversational Dutch/German/Afrikaans/Swahili.

The opening paragraph will reflect your U.S.P and your purpose statement (as covered in the first module of this book)

This section, below, contains your technical skills (as covered in the first module of this book)

This section, is self explanatory, starting with your most recent position

Always include a brief summary about the company you work(ed) for

Below your title, you will introduce a summary of your achievements

Here, you quantify your achievements

The remainder of the resume, going back in chronological time, will reflect the same format as above

Regarding your early career, be brief, and only insert a summary of achievements

Visual Appearance of Your Resume

- The fonts, the layout, the well-organized content, all contribute to the way you are perceived by the organization.
- Double and triple check your documents for any mistakes and extraneous information that will detract from your professionalism
- Use a standard typeface that is easy to read
- Use highlighted headlines in bold face type to make the resume easy to follow.
- Allow sufficient white space and margins to make it more appealing to read.
- Use bullet points and indents to set off accomplishments or to add emphasis.

Additional Tips

- Length of resume, from 2 pages to 4 pages
- How many years? Only cover 12 to 15 years
- Anything "older" than this, only use, if outstanding
- Anything older than 15 years, do not use dates

AT THE END OF THIS MODULE YOU WILL FIND

- The full resume example
- Descriptive List Table for Skills, which you can use as a guide, or prompt.

How to Write a Cover Letter

A cover letter should ALWAYS accompany your resume and serves as a formal introduction of you to a potential employer. It will inform the employer of your valuable skills and personal attributes, relating to a particular existing position or to a position you wish to create.

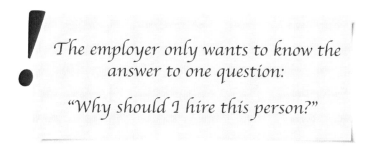

The employer only wants to know the answer to one question:

"Why should I hire this person?"

Your covering letter must do what the resume can't do. It must give the employer something to think about, that will **personalise** your interest in for the position for which you are applying and present your qualifications aligned with that position.

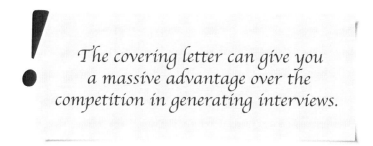

The covering letter can give you a massive advantage over the competition in generating interviews.

Covering letters are written for one of two reasons, to respond to an advertisement, or as part of your career transition strategy.

Cover Letter to Advertised Positions

Most people, including executives and professionals, turn automatically to the Employment section of their newspapers when looking for a position.

It then stands to reason, that the numbers of applicants will be quite high.

Nevertheless, for most executives, advertised positions will offer some opportunities.

Be prepared to respond to a number of advertisements without necessarily achieving particularly satisfying results.

However, you can enhance your chances, by applying simple strategies, some of which we have covered with your resume writing, targeting specific positions, and specific companies and in this section, the cover letter.

There are three types of advertisements to which you can apply:

1. Positions advertised by the companies themselves.
2. Blind advertisements
3. Recruitment consultants advertisements

Company Advertisement

Here is an excellent opportunity for researching the organisation, the name of the hiring executive and adjusting your cover letter accordingly.

Blind Advertisement

This can present some challenges, but is still representing a certain percentage of situations when a company needs to retain confidentiality, because the present incumbent might still hold the role, or they wish to keep the competition in the dark.

Recruiters Advertisement

You can enhance your chances with a preliminary enquiring telephone conversation, AFTER you have highlighted RELEVANT information about yourself.

Be well prepared before you make your call, as you may be assessed over the telephone. When handled strategically, this preparation can greatly support your subsequent cover letter writing.

Cover Letter to Unsolicited Applications

The great majority of all positions at executive levels are never advertised. One of the ways to approach them is to master the art of networking. Doing so will give you immense advantages. Networking is unquestionably one of the most important skills for you to master.

This will be covered in detail in the Hidden Market Skills module. Indeed there will be times when you will KNOW that you have specific skills that would be invaluable to an employer, or when an employer is, or will be in need for a set of skills that you can offer.

These are greatly advantageous opportunities and your approach, using networking techniques will ensure you get the chance to meet face to face with the appropriate executive.

More about this further on.

Your Covering Letter

Your goal in responding to an advertisement is simply to obtain an interview.

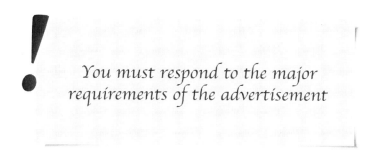

You must respond to the major requirements of the advertisement

Remember that your cover letter is a SELLING letter.

Always cover the "MUST HAVES", followed by the "nice to haves".

Always conduct as much research as possible.

If you happen not to have one of the "must haves", DO NOT rule yourself out.

It is a rare person who will meet ALL the requirements an advertiser has in mind, and the person who is finally hired will probably not do so.

Successful Techniques – Do's and Don'ts

Regardless of how proficient you may be at writing business letters or proposal, often there seems to be a struggle when contemplating a career transition letter.

Using some of the following guidelines will enhance your chances:

- You must conduct some research first to find out what is unique and special about that organisation
- Do convey genuine interest in the company and the position
- Do use an arresting introduction. This could be a statement of your strongest qualification for the position.
- Do use highly descriptive and persuasive sentences.
- Do use your strongest selling points, as relevant to the advertisement or the position you wish to create. This is not the time to be modest.
- Don't be afraid to repeat some of the achievement in your resume provided they are relevant, but alter the wording wherever possible
- Be succinct and only focus on what is of DIRECT relevance to the reader
- Focus on the employer's needs, and highlight 2-3 skills that specifically fit the position, or that would definitely be of interest for that company
- Keep it to 3 or 4 paragraphs in length.
- No longer than one page

- Address your letter to the hiring authority, including the person's correct title and business address. Call the company to and find out the name of the right person
- Do identify your correspondence as "Private and Confidential"
- Avoid overusing the "I" word. Remember, this is about the employer's needs, not yours.
- Don't mention disadvantages or weaknesses which may detract from your chances of getting the interview
- Don't mention that you are unemployed or that you have been retrenched, if this is the case
- Be polite and professional. Thank the employer/hiring manager for their time and consideration.
- Do ask for the interview. This is the "close" and a basic in successful selling. Request a "personal meeting", rather than an interview.
- Keep a record of all correspondence sent as well as advertisements responded to, so that you will be able to maintain an effective follow-up program.

Example Letters

Following are a few examples of covering letter and whilst fictitious, do reflect real life situations.

Response to an Advertisement – Example 1

Chief Executive

PRIVATE AND CONFIDENTIAL

Dear

Re: Managing Director Ref. 209B

As Chief Executive Officer of a $50 Million business, I developed an outstanding record of innovation and a reputation for raising standards and increasing profitability in a company that has become known as a leader in the industry.

My experience is exceptionally relevant to the requirements of the position you advertised. During a six year period, the company I headed accomplished the following:

- Increased sales from $12 Million to over $35 Million.
- Changed direction to take advantage of new opportunities and abandon those that were no longer attractive
- Reduced staff numbers by 18% over three years, but increased productivity, without adversely affecting morale
- Won international recognition for products we engineered
- Increased return on assets by over 180%
- Increased profit by over 250%

As you will note from the attached resume, I have always moved on to larger responsibilities, and have been successful in every instance.

The challenge of the position advertised is exciting to me. I look forward to hearing from you, and to the opportunity to meet personally.

Yours sincerely,

....

Response to an Advertisement – Example 2

Marketing Manager

PRIVATE AND CONFIDENTIAL

Dear

Re: Marketing Manager Ref. 895 C

I have been a Marketing Manager for 5 years and have had a broad experience in pharmaceuticals and chemicals.

I have achieved an annual increase of 12% in turnover and 15% in profit before interest and tax.

My abilities include the following:

- Analysing and planning skills that have led to identification of substantial new business opportunities
- Direction of successful entries into new markets, including product positioning and pricing
- Planning and managing advertising support
- Line marketing management with both sales and Profit and Loss responsibility

You may also be interested in my experience in feasibility studies and market research, whether as an integral part of my job, or as a project leader of a multi-disciplined group.

Amongst my personal qualities are creativity, a capacity for "getting things done", good inter-personal skills with dealers and customers and a good feel for maximising profit contribution

I look forward to discussing with you the contribution I can make to the further growth and success of Winning Pharmaceuticals.

Yours sincerely,

. . . .

Response to an Advertisement – Example 3

Regional Sales Manager

PRIVATE AND CONFIDENTIAL

Dear

Re: Regional Sales Manager Ref. 291 G

As a Regional Sales Manager for a consumer products company, I have a track record that I believe merits your attention. My accomplishments and skills include the following:

- Increased sales and profits in an established market and region by 42% and 53% respectively, in the first year after taking up the management role
- In a larger responsibility, turned a losing operation into one generating a $520,000 annual profit, in less than 2 years
- Experienced in management of staff, including hiring, training and motivation of up to seven sales people
- Strong abilities in budgeting and forecasting
- Increasing account penetration has been a particular strength, both during my time as a sales representative and subsequently. Recognised for superior performance in this area on a number of occasions.
- Well versed in all aspects of consumer products sales, having been responsible for managing both territories and staff for over twelve years.

I will be happy to discuss my experience and qualifications further in a personal meeting.

Yours sincerely,

....

The Follow Up Letter

This letter presents a superb opportunity to favourably differentiate yourself from the competition.

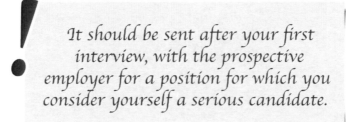

It should be sent after your first interview, with the prospective employer for a position for which you consider yourself a serious candidate.

Like the covering letter, it should be carefully customised to meet the needs of the situation. Many of the techniques applicable to the covering letter are also applicable to the follow up letter.

The follow up letter is designed to advance the interview process, or to help in generating a job offer. It is a vital supporting role in your career transition as much as it offers the potential to stand you apart from other applicants.

It will also keep your name in front of the decision maker and personalise your relationship.

Some important points to implement:

- Send it straight away after your interview. The following day at the latest
- You must convey that:

1. You paid attention
2. You understood the importance of the interviewer's/executive's comment
3. You are excited about the job. You can do it. You want it.
4. You can make an immediate contribution and your mind is already focused on the challenges

- Address the letter to the main interviewer and if they were others involved, send them a copy with a note of thanks
- Keep it short. One page maximum
- Do address the following:

1. Appreciation - for the time taken by the interviewer to meet with you
2. Challenge – you perceive the role as being interesting and challenging and you are confident in meeting the challenge
3. Interest – Express your interest in the position – You are still in selling mode
4. Impression – mention that you were impressed with the people/product/service/facility/market/positioning of the company, but don't overdo it.
5. Enthusiasm – Will make you stand out!

Example Letters

Following are a few examples of follow-up letters that you may wish to use as a guide.

Follow Up Letter – Example 1

PRIVATE AND CONFIDENTIAL

Dear

Thank you for the time you took for our meeting today. The position we discussed sounds exceptionally challenging and interesting to me. I was particularly impressed by the enthusiasm of all three of the executives with whom I spoke – Mr. Smith, Ms. Harrison and yourself, for the role of the Engineer Manager with Ideal Manufacturing Ltd.

Since you plan to reach a decision fairly quickly, I would like to restate some of the attributes that I believe particularly qualify me for the position:

- Ability to successfully manage a number of projects simultaneously
- Experience in related production engineering roles
- A record of successfully working with people at all levels of management, within a large and diverse organisation
- Proven team building abilities
- An understanding of the problems faced by the engineering function in a complex situation such as yours, and a record of solving such problems
- Strong motivation to perform at an outstanding level in any role I undertake

I enjoyed our meeting, and look forward to hearing further from you in the near future.

Yours sincerely,

....

Follow Up Letter – Example 2

PRIVATE AND CONFIDENTIAL

Dear

It was both instructive and enjoyable to meet with you today. I am confident of my ability to make an immediate contribution in the role of General Manager, and am excited about doing so.

My credentials as a results-oriented General Manager as well established. However, I feel it would be useful to comment specifically of several of the needs we discussed, and on my qualifications for meeting them.

- You indicated that problems had been encountered with regard to loss of business from several key accounts. In my earlier role in sales management with Brilliant and Remarkable, I was able to rebuild the volume of a number of accounts that had fallen off badly. Careful planning and execution in regard to one account led to rebuilding a sales volume that had fallen from over $1.5 Million to $340,000 to a level higher than ever before, within 2 years.
- You commented on the need for further staff reductions, whilst noting that it was imperative that market share be maintained. In my role as general manager at Magnus Products, I was charged with maintaining sales whilst reducing staff numbers by over 20%. The staff reduction was completed in just over 10 months, and sales increased by 12 % during this difficult period.
- As you mentioned, it will be essential to recapture the team spirit that was responsible for so much of Maximum's success in the 1990's. I have developed a reputation as a strong team builder, a fact that will be confirmed by my references.

Once again, thank you for your time. I am most interested in the position, and look forward to our further meetings.

Yours sincerely

. . . .

Descriptives for Skills Categories for Your Resume

Communication/People Skills

Addressed	Advertised	Arbitrated	Arranged
Articulated	Authored	Clarified	Collaborated
Communicated	Composed	Condensed	Conferred
Consulted	Contacted	Conveyed	Convinced
Corresponded	Debated	Defined	Developed
Directed	Discussed	Drafted	Edited
Elicited	Enlisted	Explained	Expressed
Formulated	Furnished	Incorporated	Influenced
Interacted	Interpreted	Interviewed	Involved
Joined	Judged	Lectured	Listened
Marketed	Mediated	Moderated	Negotiated
Observed	Outlined	Participated	Persuaded
Presented	Promoted	Proposed	Publicized
Reconciled	Recruited	Referred	Reinforced
Reported	Resolved	Responded	Solicited
Specified	Spoke	Suggested	Summarized
Synthesized	Translated	Wrote	

Creative Skills

Acted	Adapted	Began	Combined
Composed	Conceptualized	Condensed	Created
Customized	Designed	Developed	Directed
Displayed	Drew	Entertained	Established
Fashioned	Formulated	Founded	Illustrated
Initiated	Instituted	Integrated	Introduced
Invented	Modelled	Modified	Originated
Performed	Photographed	Planned	Revised
Revitalized	Shaped	Solved	

Data/Financial Skills

Administered	Adjusted	Allocated	Analysed
Appraised	Assessed	Audited	Balanced
Budgeted	Calculated	Computed	Conserved
Corrected	Determined	Developed	Estimated
Forecasted	Managed	Marketed	Measured
Netted	Planned	Prepared	Programmed
Projected	Qualified	Reconciled	Reduced
Researched	Retrieved		

Helping Skills

Adapted	Advocated	Aided	Answered
Arranged	Assessed	Assisted	Clarified
Coached	Collaborated	Contributed	Cooperated
Counselled	Demonstrated	Diagnosed	Educated
Encouraged	Ensured	Expedited	Facilitated
Familiarized	Furthered	Guided	Helped
Insured	Intervened	Motivated	Prevented
Provided	Referred	Rehabilitated	Represented
Resolved	Simplified	Supplied	Supported
Volunteered			

Management/Leadership Skills

Administered	Analysed	Appointed	Approved
Assigned	Attained	Authorized	Chaired
Considered	Consolidated	Contracted	Controlled
Converted	Coordinated	Decided	Delegated
Developed	Directed	Eliminated	Emphasized
Enforced	Enhanced	Established	Executed
Generated	Handled	Headed	Hired
Hosted	Improved	Incorporated	Increased
Initiated	Inspected	Instituted	Led
Managed	Merged	Motivated	Navigated
Organized	Originated	Overhauled	Oversaw
Planned	Presided	Prioritized	Produced
Recommended	Reorganized	Replaced	Restored
Reviewed	Scheduled	Secured	Selected
Streamlined	Strengthened	Supervised	Terminated

Organizational Skills

Approved	Arranged	Catalogued	Categorized
Charted	Classified	Coded	Collected
Compiled	Corrected	Corresponded	Distributed
Executed	Filed	Generated	Incorporated
Inspected	Logged	Maintained	Monitored
Obtained	Operated	Ordered	Organized
Prepared	Processed	Provided	Purchased
Recorded	Registered	Reserved	Responded
Reviewed	Routed	Scheduled	Screened
Submitted	Supplied	Standardized	Systematized
Updated	Validated	Verified	

Research Skills

Analysed	Clarified	Collected	Compared
Conducted	Critiqued	Detected	Determined
Diagnosed	Evaluated	Examined	Experimented
Explored	Extracted	Formulated	Gathered
Inspected	Interviewed	Invented	Investigated
Located	Measured	Organized	Researched
Reviewed	Searched	Solved	Summarized
Surveyed	Systematized	Tested	

Teaching Skills

Adapted	Advised	Clarified	Coached
Communicated	Conducted	Coordinated	Coordinated
Developed	Enabled	Encouraged	Evaluated
Explained	Facilitated	Focused	Guided
Individualized	Informed	Instilled	Instructed
Motivated	Persuaded	Simulated	Stimulated
Taught	Tested	Trained	Transmitted
Tutored			

Technical Skills

Adapted	Applied	Assembled	Built
Calculated	Computed	Conserved	Constructed
Converted	Debugged	Designed	Determined
Developed	Engineered	Fabricated	Fortified
Installed	Maintained	Operated	Overhauled
Printed	Programmed	Rectified	Regulated
Remodelled	Repaired	Replaced	Restored
Solved	Specialized	Standardized	Studied
Upgraded	Utilized		

Summary of Personal Qualities

Achieving	Dependent	Introverted	Self-centred
Adaptable	Diplomatic	Intuitive	Self-confident
Adventurous	Dominant	Inventive	Self-controlled
Aggressive	Dynamic	Loyal	Self-disciplined
Alert	Easy-going	Meticulous	Self-reliant
Ambitious	Efficient	Nice	Sensitive
Amiable	Emotional	Obstinate	Sentimental
Argumentative	Empathetic	Organized	Serious
Assertive	Energetic	Open-minded	Shy
Blunt	Enthusiastic	Opportunistic	Sincere
Boastful	Extroverted	Optimistic	Sociable
Calm	Fair	Orderly	Spontaneous

Cautious	Fearful	Original	Stubborn
Charitable	Firm	Outgoing	Sympathetic
Cheerful	Flexible	Outspoken	Systematic
Competitive	Forceful	Passive	Tactful
Confident	Frank	Patient	Talkative
Confused	Fussy	Persevering	Thorough
Congenial	Generous	Persuasive	Tolerant
Co-operative	Good judge	Pessimistic	Tough
Conscientious	Good-natured	Poised	Trusting
Courteous	Helpful	Polished	Trustworthy
Creative	Honest	Polite	Uncertain
Critical	Humourless	Practical	Understanding
Curious	Idealistic	Punctual	Urbane
Daring	Imaginative	Quiet	Versatile
Decisive	Independent	Reliable	Worrying
Deceptive	Industrious	Reserves	
Demanding	Ingenious	Responsible	
Dependable	Impatient	Resourceful	

If applied to an advertisement:

APPLICATION RECORD

Attach copy of advertisement

Date advertised _____ Source _____

	DATE	CONTACT	COMMENTS
Phone Inquiry/ Email reply			
Letter/Resume			
Follow up call			
1st Interview			
F/U Letter			
2nd Interview			
F/U Letter			
3rd Interview			
F/U Letter			
Other:			

If approached directly

CAREER SEARCH RECORD

ACTIVITY	Week Ending:				
	Mon	Tues	Wed	Thu	Fri
Networking: Initial					
Phone calls					
Meetings					
Referrals					
Interviews					
Results/ Feed Back					
Networking: Follow Up					
Phone calls					
Referrals					
Interviews					
Results/ Feed Back					
Positions Advertised					
Preliminary phone calls					
Applications sent					
Interviews					
Results/ Feed back					
Consultant/Agents					
Contacts					
Resume sent					
Follow ups					
Interviews					
Results/ Feedback					

INTERVIEW ASSESSEMENT

Company _____   DATE: _____

Contact/s: _____   PHONE: _____

	Comments / Rating 1 - 5
About the company:	
About the interviewers	
About my Research/ Preparation	
About the Interview:	
About perceived challenging questions:	
How well did I present?	
What went well?	
What was difficult?	
General Comments/Future Actions	
Other	

Preparing for the Interview

How Do You Sell Yourself when You Are Not a Sales Person?

In order to develop a successful executive or professional career, it is important to learn how to sell one's abilities to solve the problems of an employer. It is even more important today than ever before and those who cannot learn this process suffer in their career at every level. It is well worth going through the discomfort of the learning process in order not to be denied more stimulating opportunities that could be theirs, together with the increased compensations that accompany them.

Selling oneself provides a sense of mastery and control over one's career that is well worth learning.

Why do we find it so hard to sell ourselves? We can speak of something, somewhere, someone quite eloquently. Anything outside of ourselves seems so easy and effortless.

But when it comes to ourselves, it is more difficult, isn't it?

There are only 2 blocks to interview success that most people experience;

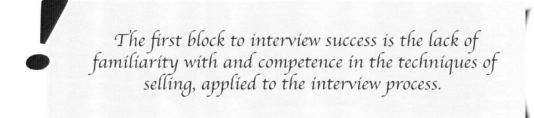

The first block to interview success is the lack of familiarity with and competence in the techniques of selling, applied to the interview process.

This is covered in the ECMS Interview Skills module.

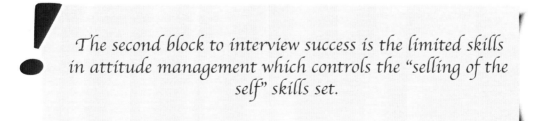

The second block to interview success is the limited skills in attitude management which controls the "selling of the self" skills set.

Obviously, as an executive, you already possess considerable skills in attitude management. This is crucial in regard to selling yourself and this is the area we will concentrate on in this section.

Why Is Positive Attitude to Yourself So Important?

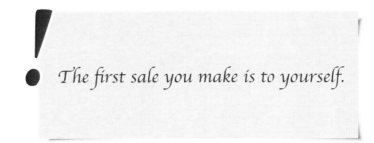

The first sale you make is to yourself.

Firstly you need to be convinced that you are right for the role you apply for. Then it will be easier to market your ability to contribute to the organization.

If you are not totally sold on the value to an employer of your services, it will be difficult to make the sale.

Enthusiasm is infectious and sales are only made in a positive environment, not only towards the employer, the interview situation, but to yourself first!

The secret of getting ahead, of obtaining the competitive edge, is your ability to persuade potential employers that they need you.

That's what selling is all about.

A professional salesperson is a confident, knowledgeable problem solver. Selling is an art that, once learned, can benefit you for the rest of your life -- and get you the jobs you want.

Who You Are Sells Itself

The person who sells themselves with integrity will see work as an opportunity to make a contribution of lasting value and one who views management as a commitment to enrich others.

Once your preparation for the interview is complete, you can just be yourself.

Once you are fully integrated within yourself, the "selling of yourself" will happen automatically. Ralph Waldo Emerson said it brilliantly:"What you are shouts so loudly in my ears, I can't hear a word you're saying"

Your personal integrity is central to the buyer's decision-making process. It shows itself of greater importance than ability, even though the interview is based on ability and experience questioning and discussions.

A Little Self- Assessment

A career move is an infrequent event, for most of us, but when it occurs, it is a good time to reflect on where we are headed and why?

To know what you want to do is a good starting point.

Who do you want to work for? Anyone/Any company in particular?

How do you want to go about building the next phase of your career?

When do you want to make your next move?

Most importantly WHY do you want to make a career move?

Is your motivation primarily based on a need to attain financial security, or do you also see your work as an opportunity to contribute to society?

Of course, you will be more attractive to an employer who knows he can trust you to act professionally, because he/she knows that you are committed to doing the right thing, rather than pursuing your own agenda.

More and more corporations are looking for leaders – intelligent people who are able to influence other intelligent people because their motivation for working is based on their values in life, which are based on principles. You will find this attitudinal approach to be a good formula for career transition success.

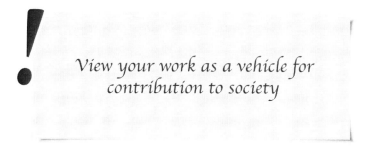

> View your work as a vehicle for contribution to society

This will present you in a different way to competitive candidates and engender confidence in your application.

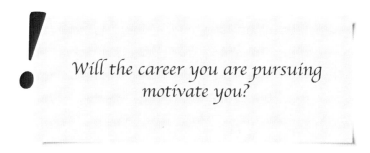

> Will the career you are pursuing motivate you?

You will find that once you have clarified your values and your mission in life, you will be in a much better position to set goals that will motivate you and that will enable you to influence others.

- Please review the section on Your Personal Mission Statement.
- Please review the section on your Career Goals

Review the above before an interview, as you will find them useful to respond and participate to the interview process with the utmost integrity.

Your List of Positive Characteristics

The following list of positive characteristics will maximise your chances of getting the job you seek.

How many of these characteristics do you have?

- Are you motivated and realistically enthusiastic?
- Do you initiate opportunities where none seems to exist?
- Do you speak highly about your own capabilities?
- Do you seize the opportunity when you see a chance to put yourself forward for an employment or career advancement possibility?
- Do you answer all questions confidently and welcome them as opportunities?
- Do you shut your mind tight against negative influences from media, family and friends?
- Do you present yourself well?
- Are you able to present yourself at a moment's notice?
- Do you welcome the chance to speak with confidence before a group, such as panel interviews or workshops?
- Do you act and speak with confidence even when you have to resort to saying:" I don't know, but I will certainly find out!"?
- Do you resist the temptation to put others down so that you feel better by comparison?

If you score at least 8, you are on your way to successfully securing the next position of your choice!

If you perceive that you have scored rather well, but feel you are still not making progress in the right direction, review your motivation, your vision and your goals.

It might just be a lack of focus in those areas.

The reality is that unless you are prepared to go further than other people, unless you turn over every stone, you may not make it.

You cannot allow yourself to be talked out of using every tool at your disposal and exploring every option.

You have to tackle every set-back as early as possible, before it grows on you. If you let it, it will undermine all your efforts and show up in your application letter or the way you express yourself at your next interview.

This is important!

Determine to use the positive power of your mind to maximum effect during your job search. Get yourself into a positive attitude and maintain it.

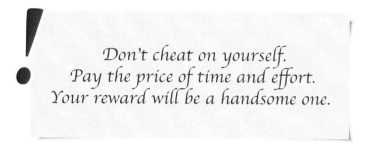

Don't cheat on yourself.
Pay the price of time and effort.
Your reward will be a handsome one.

Some Good Tips

- Don't panic. You are on your way to the next stage in your life.
- Have faith in working your plan. Invest time, be thorough and committed to your goals. Yourself worth is dependent on this and will get stronger as you work your plan.
- Allow yourself to be human. Feel free to vent your frustration along the way.
- Get some help if you get depressed
- If you need to talk, TALK. Do not suppress your emotions.
- Remember your assets and be aware of your limitations. Be objective and realistic about your goals.
- Look for things that you really enjoy and find satisfaction in your life.
- Make your job search interesting and enjoyable, not something to be endured
- Sleep more; it will revitalise you and give you renewed energy.
- Exercise; you will need to be the best you can be.
- Grooming; do pay special attention to this. Pamper yourself. The better you feel the better your mindset.
- WORK... throw yourself into your program like your life depends on it. Your quality of life does depend on it!

Remember that getting employed or re-employed is a numbers game. That means that there are more people who will say NO to you than YES.

With this, you MUST also remember NEVER to take rejection personally.

It would support you better to react the following way:

- That was a good dry run. I have learned something from that. Next time will be better
- It costs very little to try. You have to be in it to win. I will keep working at it.

Knowing this is good, but when you DO something practical, it is much better.

Give Yourself Every Chance

Manage your time effectively in following these tips:

- Treat your job search as a career in itself. Keep yourself busy in the pursuit of your goal. If you are unemployed, put in 40 hours a week UNTIL you have accepted a position offer.
- Work on your self-image. Work on a fitness campaign for yourself, it will show up positively at the interviews.
- Remain professional at all times
- Ensure that you keep good records of your search activities.
- Give yourself time to relax. You must maintain some balance in your life and take rest on weekends, so that you don't turn up stressed out at interviews.
- Contact every lead
- Research every company you contact. This will give you an advantage over your competition
- Do the numbers. It is a numbers game. It is a sales process. Never back off. Go the extra mile. You only need one YES !
- Work smart. Pick your mark.
- Keep positive. Concentrate on your successes and let that energy come through your phone calls and your interviews.
- Feel good about yourself and practice visualising yourself getting that position.

Remember also, that most top positions are never advertised. They are never seen by most potential applicants. And whilst you can choose to restrict yourself to advertised positions only, this will limit your chances. We will cover how to access the Hidden Market in a further module.

Remember also, all you need is ONE (right) position.

How to Visualise GETTING that Position

The first step is to get into a state of relaxation, then to create a vision of what it would be like to be offered that coveted position.

Find a place that is quiet, where you will not have any interruptions. A quiet room or somewhere in nature. Be as present to where you are as much as possible: if you are in nature, with your body feeling the breeze on your skin, or the sun warming your back, or the smell of the trees, or the smell of the salt of the ocean if you are close to the beach.

Take slow deep breaths, for a few minutes. Then imagine that you have a few party balloons, of different colours, blue, red, yellow, green, floating above your head. Imagine that you put your worrying thoughts inside these balloons, each type of worry in a different colour balloon, until you feel that your head has empties all your worries into them.

Then release them and watch the breeze take them away, as they rise into the sky, higher and higher, until you no longer can even see them.

Now, imagine your closest friends being around you, perhaps at a celebratory dinner occasion, where you talk to them and they are reminding you of your successes and your greatest work achievements. You are feeling relaxed and happy and reminiscent about your accomplishments. You are reliving them with your supporting friends and remember how great you felt and you now feel great as well.

And now your friends are gently walking away from the scene, and you find yourself in an office with a smiling senior executive who is shaking you warmly by the hand, congratulating you on been appointed to their company.

> *Feel the strong handshake.*
> *See the warm welcoming eyes.*
> *Feel the sincerity and the eager invitation as you delightedly accept.*
> *Feel the excitement of it, as you want to rush and tell the good news to your friends and your family.*

Do this exercise every night before you go to sleep and every morning when you wake up. This is when you are the most relaxed. It will align your conscious and subconscious mind and will give you renewed calm and confidence.

Final Tips and Summary

- Don't waste time:
- If you are employed – set aside time regularly each week for the job search.
- If you are unemployed – make your job search your full-time job
- Use spare time for self-improvement – reading – exercising – It will show through at the interview
- Your wardrobe must be READY, at all times for that important interview. Plan ahead.
- Have your "Interview Kit" at the ready. You will need 2 copies of your resume, a list of questions you are likely to want to ask, a writing pad, written references, newspaper articles, or examples of past successes
- Research THOROUGHLY the company who invites you for an interview. Also research the industry, the competitors, the culture
- Know how long it will take you to get to the venue where the interview will take place.

The "ECMS" System for Interview Success

This section contains areas to meet differing requirements regarding interviewing skills.

It will:

- Increase your understanding of how you affect interviewers and help you to see how your personal presentation can be made more effective
- Show you how to master the "inner game" of selling yourself at the interview
- Enable you to effectively handle stressful questions often posed by employers or consultants and to be at ease in even the most challenging of interview situations
- Provide you with the specific selling techniques required to outperform the competition at every stage of the interview process and reinforce them through practice and role play
- Show you how to handle difficult situations such as interruptions during an interview and dealing with the untrained interviewer and how to maintain control in a panel interview situation
- Set out what you MUST do and must NOT do, after the interview

About ECMS: Effective Career Management System

The Essentials for Your Interview Success

There are two essentials for your interview success.

1. **The techniques:**
   - Sharpening your presentation skills and clarifying the psychology and methodology of the recruitment process
   - Exposing emotions revealed by body language in an interview
   - Helping you counter stressful questions often posed by employers and consultants
   - Identifying requirements for effective salary negotiations
   - Overcoming the effect of interruptions during an interview
   - Explaining how to maintain control in a panel interview situation

2. **The "Inner game":**
   - Developing and maintaining the winning values, beliefs, goals, plans, attitudes and motivation required for successful career transition.
   - This is about *living life on your terms.*

You probably never would have achieved management level responsibility in the first place unless you already had a good understanding of the primary importance of factors such as goals and motivation, of course. But it's important to review them in the context of your career transition.

We will cover:

- Preparing for the Interview
- Selling yourself at the Interview
- Mastering Interview Questions

Making The Most Of The Interview Skills Modules

You can either put your heart and soul into this module and get the maximum value from it or make excuses for not doing so. Determine to do the former. You will be able to tell the difference, so will interviewers. Most importantly though, doing so will positively affect your life.

Mock up Workshop

There will be a workshop module available separately to this book for corporations, as well as videos. In this book though, we will duplicate the same exercises which can be done by yourself. It is more difficult, and will require more effort and discipline but you will find the results extremely rewarding.

Threat these exercises as the "Real Thing" rather than "just practice" and determine to give your very best performance. We are not seeking to make you the ultimate presenter, but

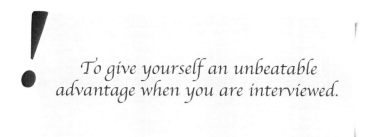

To give yourself an unbeatable advantage when you are interviewed.

That requires **preparation** and **practice** on your part.

Allocate a room in your house or area in your office, where you will practice presentations and mock interviews, then enrol the help of a friend that you can subsequently present this to.

Set up a time in your diary for practising and adhere to it.

When the time arrives for you to give your presentation, be ready! Be thoroughly familiar with this written material.

There will be hundreds of excuses for avoiding entering into this exercise, but if you commit to present to a friend(s), it will be an excellent way to simulate the real life demands and uncertainties of the interview situation.

GIVE YOUR PRESENTATION WHEN IT IS DUE. Don't cheat yourself or the friend you have chosen for this exercise.

All of the principles you have to use for this exercise can be applied and used on a daily basis. Positive thinking, how to think and present logically, how to positively influence others, are all things that can be sharpened continually.

We suggest that the first presentation and mock-up interview that you prepare would be by yourself, then a day or a week later at the latest, be ready to present to your friend. Lock it into your diary.

It is best when making this presentation to your friend that it is not done in a restaurant, or coffee shop, or the pub. It is best to have an environment that closely resembles the REAL situation you will be invited to present in. This is important, as it will "anchor" the situation in your subconscious mind ready to be re-enacted with ease when the situation calls for it in real life.

When you present to your friend, do dress as though you were really going for an interview. This will make it more authentic and ensure you are prepared when an interview opportunity presents itself and will thus heighten the value of this preparation to you.

Introductions / Discussion Points

Imagine that you are called upon to express your ideas on a given subject, perhaps in the realm of current affairs, in order to strengthen the skill of expressing ideas briefly and convincingly.

The purpose of this exercise is for you to learn to collect your thoughts when under pressure, and present your response logically and convincingly without embarrassment or awkwardness.

Subjects that are probably of interest to potential employers and interviewers, would be economy related subjects, industry related subjects or any current affairs subjects that could be of interest to explore and debate.

Each subject can be like a short impromptu speech. It is your chance to practice and strengthen your ability to think on your feet.

Imagine comments at least a couple of comments that could be made, which would require further explanation from yourself. Try to have an answer for every question asked.

Regarding the interview questions, avoid long answers. Remember that the interview offers a very limited opportunity to sell yourself, and it is imperative that you make the most of every moment.

For most interview questions, you should only speak for a minute or so. Do time your Introduction, and your responses to make you more conscious of this important element of successful interview technique. The time allocated for responses to particular discussion points may vary in real life, however use one minute per question, as a general rule.

Make your comments clear and concise. Obviously, you will need to be informed on what is going on in the world. Think about the issues that are on thinking people's minds. Be able to back up your comments with logic or proof. Be prepared to speak out on the subjects raised but don't forget to remain diplomatic.

Remember that you will only get out of the session what you put into it. The key to success in this mock up exercise, as in life, is PREPARATION and PARTICIPATION.

Presentations and Evaluations

The value you receive from this major portion of the program doubles and redoubles when you fully involve yourself. You not only learn to present by presenting, you will grow in awareness of what works and what doesn't . You will be amazed with your improvements.

Here's how it works. We allow four minutes for each presentation. Have a kitchen timer with you, or use the alarm of your watch and set it for 3 minutes. When it rings, you will know that you have only one minute left.

If you have a hand held video recorder, tape yourself, then watch yourself.

Evaluate your presentation and do it again, until you are happy with it.

You can show it to a friend, and ask their opinion as well.

Don't forget, you are not an actor, you are an executive who wants to make a persuasive professional presentation.

Next time you listen to the News, or any TV presenter, sit up and really take notice.

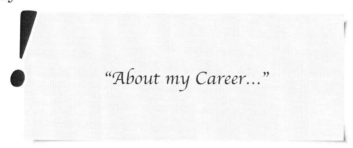

You will be amazed how many tips you will pick up by actively watching others.

Don't be too hard on yourself, just learn and practice. It **is** an opportunity to learn and grow.

Your First Delivery

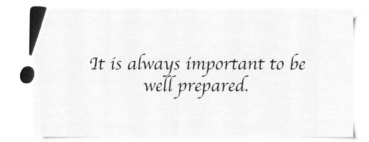

"About my Career…"

This is your chance to speak about your accomplishments. Whilst it is important to stay with the facts, as this presentation is preparing you for the interview but definitely not the time to be modest. Let your accomplishments shine brightly. Speak to your audience as if you were addressing a panel of interviewers. Giving this presentation will prepare you to give any interviewer a tightly structured synopsis of your background and accomplishments. And just as importantly, it will give you the opportunity to learn how you come across to others.

Preparation

It is always important to be well prepared.

So, here are a few tips:

1. Prepare yourself to answer broad questions like: "Tell me about yourself"
2. It is quite normal if you are experiencing nervousness about delivering your first presentation. Most people feel nervous when addressing a group of people. The more you prepare and practice, the less nervous you will be at the interview itself.
3. The reality is that most people waste the opportunity to sell themselves effectively at the interview. This exercise will give you the opportunity to achieve a level of preparation that will make you as effective as possible at the interview.

Now get organised;

- Write down the main points you want to present.
- Be sure you have a logical arrangement of ideas or a story flow.
- Concentrate on one central theme.
- Select a point you will use to open your delivery and one to conclude with. Get each of these points clear in your mind, because it is better to give your presentation without notes. If you need notes, only use point form as a prompter.

You will find that practice will make it easier for you and you will notice getting better with it. Rehearsing your presentation a couple of times before giving it will give you more support and confidence as well. Practice until you hear yourself saying the words.

Your Pitch

When you give your first presentation, you would probably start with telling the audience about your career to date. Scan the audience, greet them, then talk to the whole group and tell them about yourself. Have eye contact with one, then another member of the audience, and so on, and talk to them personally, not as though you were talking to a crowd, but each as an individual.

Forget everything except what you have to communicate and the time that is allocated for your presentation and keep your delivery within this time span.

Your Second Delivery

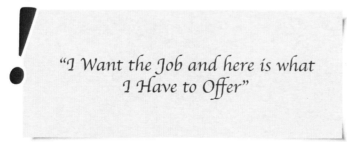

This presentation will be easier because you know your subject! Sit down quietly with your resume and think through all the positions you have filled in the past. Bring to mind all the successes and the abilities and skills you have learned to use.

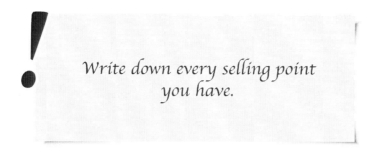

Write down every selling point you have.

Now, let's look at the realities. First impressions are absolutely crucial. Choices are made early in the interview. You will be either chosen or rejected based on these first few minutes of the interview. The remainder of the interview will be devoted to finding reasons why that decision was made.

What you need to do is work on the following basis. Your presentation has to be based on a number of assumptions:

1. You are in an interview situation.
2. Your aim is to grab the floor and use that first few minutes immediately following the introductions and development of rapport at the beginning of the interview to your advantage.
3. You could use an opening statement that allows you to get in first and talk. This could be something like:" While I was waiting in reception, I reread your job advertisement, or job description, or the information about your company. May I take a minute or so here to comment on it?" Then launch into why you fit the profile so precisely.

Of course, this is not always possible, and always respect the interviewer's own agenda, but try to do so as soon as an opportunity presents itself.

The earlier this presentation is used the better, however, it may still be used late in the meeting. This can be done, for example, in response to the question "Why should we hire you?" or to a question such as

"Is there anything else you'd like to cover?"

Put forward your selling points and put them forward powerfully for maximum effect.

You may not always get the opportunity to present what you have rehearsed, but because you have been primed, you will probably be able to use subsequent questions to pick out opportunities to continue to sell.

We will cover this in a later section of this book. For now, you need to concentrate on packaging your selling points into a three to four minute period.

Omit all unnecessary ideas, thoughts, and any waffle.

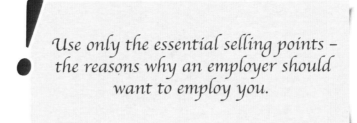

Use only the essential selling points – the reasons why an employer should want to employ you.

You should either use a real job advertisement for a position which represents what you are looking for, or describe to the "audience" the type of position and organisation you are seeking, and the likely requirements of the employer. If you use an advertisement, read it out, aloud, before your presentation, so that the "audience" can evaluate how effectively you address these requirements.

It's best to give the presentation without notes. However, you can use a word or two as prompters, on a notepad, to recall important thoughts. When you practice your presentation (and you should practice this one and polish it as much as you possibly can) jot down any key point that you have difficult recalling or working into your presentation.

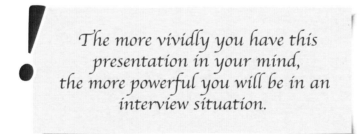

The more vividly you have this presentation in your mind, the more powerful you will be in an interview situation.

Most importantly, the clearer your mental picture of what you are going to say, the more focused your mind will be on what is most important, both to the interviewer and to your job prospects.

Get your opening statement and your closing statement clearly in mind. Picture yourself sitting across the desk from an interviewer and presenting. Hear yourself saying the words. Before dropping off to sleep, have that picture in your mind.

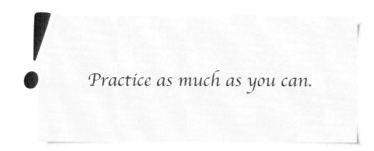

Practice as much as you can.

Your Pitch

Once you have introduced yourself, greet the audience. Pause, just a little to gain their attention. Gain positive eye contact. Single out two or three key people to whom you will talk more than to the others. Study their reactions. Make sure you keep their attention. Press your points home, but don't rush nervously. Forget yourself and concentrate on what you have to say. Make that your absolute priority. Nothing else matters.

Repetition Is the Mother of Skill

Rehearse the presentations you will be giving over and over again before actually giving them. Do the same with your answers to interview questions especially those that could be particularly troublesome to you. The **ECMS** Interview skills workshops and the video interview can yield massive benefits. But what you get out of these mock workshops either by yourself or with a friend/friends, and the Interview Skills module, will be in direct proportion to what you put into them.

Mastering Interview Questions

This section is designed to contain supporting material designed to develop and enhance interview skills, and covers subjects such as:

- The interviewer's major fears
- The warning signs: what do interviewers look for?
- Understanding the various types of interview questions, and the reasons why they are asked
- The main principles of success in handling interview questions
- How to control the interviewer's focus
- Dealing with the "stress" interviewer
- Turning stress questions into opportunities to sell yourself. How to deal with the stress questions that could destroy your chances of getting the offer.
- Practice in handling stress questions

It can happen that the interview goes really smoothly, UNTIL an unanticipated question is asked to which the interviewee doesn't know the answer, fumbles and gets off his stride. The interview that has been going so well becomes awkward and embarrassing.

It would be nice if the above scenario were an isolated one, unfortunately, this is not the case.

Of course, it doesn't have to be so. The interview doesn't have to be a journey into the unknown, with the potential for nasty surprises and it shouldn't turn into an embarrassing or unpleasant experience. It is entirely realistic to expect, with the right preparation, to sail through interviews comfortably, confidently and enjoyably.

Though they may be worded in many different ways, each of us has a limited range of questions that could pose difficulties for us in the interview. And there's no need to let them be a source of problems or stress. Success in handling interview questions comes from understanding the specific kinds of questions that could cause you difficulties and why they're asked. It involves developing responses to these questions and it involves practicing those responses until they can be delivered virtually automatically, while you concentrate on the finer points of the interaction and on continually building the rapport between you and the interviewer.

The interviewer wants to be satisfied, and your aim must be to demonstrate that you are willing, able and manageable. The questions asked are thus likely to cover much more than your technical skills and can be expected to focus also on such areas as your motivation and how well you could be expected to fit into the organisation.

> *Your job is to help the interviewer to obtain the information that he or she needs.*

To do this, it's helpful to understand the motivation behind the questions that are asked.

The Interviewer's Fears

The Interviewer's fears must be addressed and allayed before you can expect to be offered the position. You'll find they all fit under the umbrella of being **willing, able and manageable**. Here are the major ones:

1. That you might not be able to do the job (either through lack of the necessary skills or qualifications)
2. That you might be disloyal
3. That if you are hired, you may not put in the necessary level of energy required by the role
4. That you will pursue your own agenda and be unreceptive to guidance/suggestion
5. That you might not stay long enough to fulfil the company's agenda
6. That your performance might be under par to what is expected
7. That you may not show the leadership they are seeking to find
8. That you might bring discredit on them

Major warning signs for which an interviewer will be on the lookout are:

- Any signs of dishonesty or lying
- Any signs of irresponsibility or disinterest
- Any signs of arrogance or excessive aggressiveness
- Any signs of inability to meet work commitments
- Lack of willingness to be managed/ or receive suggestions from direct reports
- Complaining or blaming things on others
- Lack of motivation or enthusiasm for the Company and its goals
- Signs of instability or inappropriate responses

Remember that you will be evaluated not just on what you say, but on your body language, tone of voice and general delivery and appearance.

Types of Interview Questions

There are basic classifications under which interview questions fall under;

1. **General information and background questions.**
   These are the "easy questions" of the interview process, simply requiring information about your present situation or background. And yet it is still important to prepare in advance so you can present yourself in a way that is advantageous.

   - Tell me about yourself.
   - How do you evaluate your subordinates? Do you use any performance appraisal procedures ?
   - Describe a typical day in your present position.
   - What are the limits of your authority in your present job?

2. **Attribute and skill measurement questions.**
   These questions can be general questions, or designed to test and probe. They can range from the old standbys – general questions designed to learn as much about you as possible in the shortest possible time – to thoughtful and carefully structured questions, designed to test and probe:

   - What are your greatest strengths?
   - How do you work under pressure?
   - How would your subordinates rate you as a leader? How do you know?
   - Tell me about an experience in your career that really challenged you.

3. **"Stress" questions, or those designed specifically to expose weaknesses**
   These are potentially to expose weaknesses and thus rule you out. Do not take these personally, they are used on everyone.

   - In what respects to you feel that your last boss could have done a better job?
   - Tell me about a situation in which your work was criticised.
   - You've had a lot of job changes, haven't you? Why is that?
   - Why aren't you earning more at your age?
   - What problems do you have in getting along with others?

How to Handle Interview Questions

(Or, there are only so many tough questions you can be asked!)

Would you believe that most interviewers are as ill at ease as the interviewee? Very few are trained to handle this element of the recruitment process and they do it infrequently and poorly. This provides you with a superb opportunity to direct the discussion along lines favourable to you.

Indeed, unless you are interviewed by a well trained professional recruiter, this is going to be the case and you can turn the tables so that you can be in charge of the interview.

What is important is that you have the tools to handle whatever you need at the right time.

You could be subjected to a pressure interview, containing tricks, intimidation, subterfuge – anything to throw you off balance and allow the "real you" to be seen. Fortunately, this is not something that an inexperienced interviewer can sustain. However, you must be prepared for this kind of circumstance as well.

You will know for sure that you're facing a tough interviewer, if any of the following occurs:

- No hints
- No comments, no encouragement
- No eye contact at the start of an interview
- No greeting
- Lack of small talk
- Apparent disinterest or boredom

Don't worry about it, there are some tips in this chapter that will arm you to handle such situations.

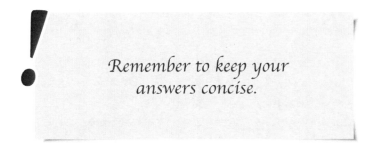

Remember to keep your answers concise.

Most questions can be answered in a minute or less. Applying this principle gives you the opportunity to achieve the maximum results within the confines of the time allocated to the interview.

It is important too, to develop skill in **closure** – the art of dealing with a question in such a way as to ensure that it can't recur or be explored further. This is partly a matter of the content of your response, and partly related to non-verbal elements of the response. For example, a downward inflection at the end of the response has the effect of tending to close the subject, whilst an upward inflection tends to invite further questions.

Another important principle to remember is this:

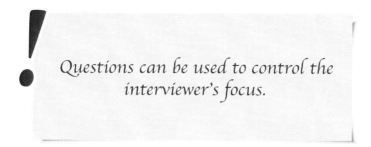

Questions can be used to control the interviewer's focus.

Often, a question can be answered and then followed up with a question of your own. Doing so will give you the opportunity to change the direction of the interview and can frequently be used to your advantage when under pressure.

Here are a few examples of the major stress questions:

What is your greatest weakness?

This is a question that can create panic in most candidates and sometimes is an invitation to self-destruct. Don't let this happen to you! All you need to do is to prepare well for this eventuality, and it will be asked of you since it is one of the classic questions.

This is probably one of the favourite stress questions so here are some options for you to use:

1. Treat the question as if it relates solely to your weaknesses relative to the job in question. Choose a minor part of the position you are applying for, where you lack that specific experience or knowledge required – but can easily overcome this very minor limitation.
2. For example, you may not have worked with a specific software package before, but you have ten years experience with 2 other very similar software packages. Obviously, you could easily install this new software on your home computer and within a week or so, you would be full up to speed with it."
3. So, with the above example, you have taken the emphasis quickly away from an apparent weakness and, in relegating it to a minor developmental problem that can be easily overcome, you have demonstrated some of your strengths.
4. Give a generalised answer that allows you to key in your value system. In other words,

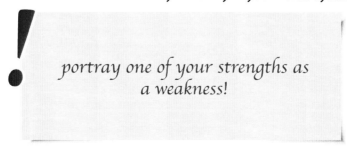

portray one of your strengths as a weakness!

For example, you could say that you enjoy work and that you usually get totally involved in what you are doing. As a result you can get a bit frustrated if you feel other people are not pulling their weight. You can further say that you are aware of the need to lead others rather than berate them, and that you make it a personal challenge to take a positive approach and to get others equally enthusiastic about whatever it is that you are collectively doing.

Of course, handle this with subtlety so that you do not appear deceptive.

1. You could relegate the problem to the past. Do take an historical weakness and show/tell how it became one of your STRENGTHS. So, you are still answering the question, but will end on a positive note.
2. For example, you could mention that you used to have a problem with your paperwork, because you did not like it you did not handle it well. Fortunately, you had a manager who walked you through the consequences from the company's viewpoint and also explained how sloppy habits would hold back your career progress. Since then you have been fastidious about your paperwork, and as a result of this, it now shows up as one of your strengths, as any referee could attest

This approach shows that you are willing to accept and act on criticism, which is a bonus. It is good to remember that

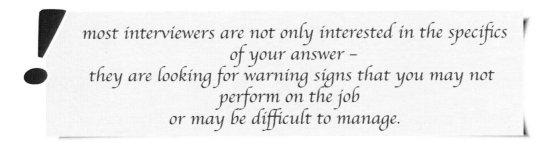

most interviewers are not only interested in the specifics of your answer –
they are looking for warning signs that you may not perform on the job
or may be difficult to manage.

Why aren't you earning more at your age?

You could treat this as a compliment.

For example, you could say that you have always felt that developing skills and experience was your top priority – and that this would stand you in good stead in the long run, and the rewards would come in due course. You could also add that you pride yourself on your loyalty to your employer and that you wouldn't change jobs just for the money.

Don't allow the interviewer a second stab at his one! Follow up your response with a question! Immediately after this statement, ask the interviewer:" With your knowledge of the industry, how much should I be earning now?" The figure given may well be the employer's package for this position.

With hindsight, how could you have improved your career progress?

This is another "Tell me about your greatest weakness" style question. Give a short answer in which you pick out skills you have learned or experience you have gained, and point out that gaining them earlier or faster, would have propelled you forward further or earlier in your career. Close the question with a final comment such as: "Apart from that, I really would not change much. I have found that experience is the teacher and I have given it my best".

Tell me about the problems you have living within your means?

This question is really designed to catch you off guard and of course your finances are nobody else's business but yours. However, this is not the response that you can give so try this one instead: "I have always been careful with my finances, set my priorities and ensure that all my bills are paid on time. This is not to say that I am satisfied with my current earnings and like any professional I'm always looking to improve my standard of living."

What kind of decision's are most difficult for you to make?

Be very careful with this one!

Most executive and professional level people have had to fire someone at some time. Most hated it. Since this is perfectly normal, this is something suitable that you can talk through. Of course you must also stress that you can and will do even the difficult things when it is for the good of the company.

What area of your professional development do you want to improve at this time?

This is another "Tell me your weaknesses" invitation

You could answer that from what you have been told about the position, you seem to have all the necessary skills and experience. Tell the interviewer that what you really find exciting about the opportunity, which is to work on a job where the salient points of the role happen to be your skills and selling points, and go through them again, which shows your enthusiasm about the job. Interviewers love it!

You can do the above, and/ or also focus in on the two greatest strengths that you bring to the position, and finish by saying:

"I think you would agree that these areas are so important that no one can be too good nor should they ever stop trying to polish their skills."

Your application shows that you have been with one company for a long time without any real increase in responsibility or salary. Why?

You will almost certainly be spared the "salary" part of this question (your salary history should not appear in your resume or covering letter) though many other candidates when faced with this question fumble it badly. The only way the interviewer will be able to ask it is if the interviewing organisation has been professional enough to have you complete a job application form which demanded that information. *If one of these forms is waved at you, do not complete this section.* If you have the qualities and abilities to do the job, and your salary progression has been unsatisfactory, no sensible employer will wave your submission because you missed this section of the application form.

If the interviewer really digs in hard on this one and insists on the information, you need to realise why. The interviewer is looking for two things:

1. Your salary rises, reflecting your performance.
2. The relative value of the offer to be made.

The important thing in these circumstances is for you to avoid any job offer being tied to your historical salary. The offer you negotiate must be based on the value of the job to the employer. This is especially important if you are a woman since women are still typically paid less than men for equal work.

> *Keep your answers about your salary situation suitably vague.*

For example, you could say that your salary has risen steadily over the years, and that you have regularly received bonus increases. Tell the interviewer that you would be happy to give the specifics if they need them but that you need to check your records at home.

It would be very rare for the interviewer to pursue matters further. Don't do anything further unless you get a second request. It would be very unusual if you were asked to give further information about this matter.

If you are really pushed to give an answer, try a different approach and tell the interviewer that one of the reasons you are currently looking for a change is that your employer takes a unilateral approach to salary increases and that either everyone gets the same percentage increase or nothing. This means that those with superior performance get the same as the other employees who are regularly underperforming. You would prefer to work in an environment where those who go above and beyond what is required are recognised.

Then put the interviewer back in the spotlight

"is this the sort of company where I can expect that?

Next, you must address the "no promotions?" element.

This part of the question is crucial. It is important to keep to absolutely essentials with this part of the question.

You could say that your current or past employer is a stable company with good working conditions but there has been virtually no growth in your department. You could push the point further by saying the there have been no promotions since …. date, or that you have been there for x years, and that you have not seen ONE single promotion in any department during this period.

Then, you can say that this question highlights the reason why you are at the interview today. Then follow through straight away with saying that you have the skills and ability to take on more responsibility, you have earned your stripes and you are looking for a place to do that."

Why have you been out of work so long?

You must be able to satisfactorily explain any and all gaps in your employment history. If you can't you are unlikely to get another job offer. Given today's employment dynamics you will have more latitude than in the past – but not much!

You need to emphasise that one of your key considerations in any time of unemployment was (is) that you were (are) not just looking for a monthly pay packet. You were (are) looking for the right sort of opportunity/ company with whom you could build a long-term future.

You could say for example that you made a conscious decision not to look just for any job, but that you are looking for job satisfaction, not another pay cheque. That you are determined that the next job you take would be one where you could settle down and do your best to make a really solid contribution. You then would say to the interviewer that from what you have heard, their company seems to expect their people to pull their own weight because you have a big job to do and that you like that, and you would like to be part of the team. Then ask "What have I got to do to get the job?"

Keep in mind that if you have been out of work and say that you have been doing consulting work, the interviewer will know it unless you can be specific about it. If this is the case, mention the name of the company or companies and what type of consulting work you were/are involved in. You could add:" This is not what I want to do long term, however it is keeping me busy right now"

Then get back to the job under discussion.

Why have you changed jobs so frequently?

If you changed jobs often when you were younger, it is forgivable, but as you mature in years, there is an expectation of stability and long term commitment. Of course, you could also say that the only way for you to grow professionally, was to change companies, to achieve the level of experience you have achieved today.

You could say for example that your first job required a lot of travel and whilst it was a good experience, you then found a job much closer to home. This job offered the chance to broaden your experience with a new company that was starting up. On hindsight, you can see now that your level of contribution was limited. So, you left to join XYZ and have been with the company now for 6 years. You could add that the different experiences you have had, have been a real advantage and that you have more experience to offer as a result of that, but still a genuine desire to settle down and make the experience pay off for yourself and your employer.

Or you can say something like:

One of the things that has been important to you is challenge. That you have a strong desire to contribute and that is why you are looking for an employer that will keep you challenged. You think you may have found that employer. Is this right?

Why did you leave your last job? Why do you want to leave your current job?

If you don't have a list of acceptable reasons already in mind, here is a list for you to choose from:

- **Lack of Challenge:** You weren't able to grow in the position.
- **No Career Advancement:** There was nowhere for you to go. You had the talent but there were simply too many people ahead of you in line for advancement.
- **Security:** The Company was not stable.
- **Low Salary:** The organisation had salary limitations and not geared to paying you what you were really worth.
- **Reputation:** You wanted to be with a better organisation, a market leader in their field, a company open to innovation, etc.

What didn't you like in your last company?

This is a question that will guide the interviewer in finding your potential "fit" for a new company, or maybe a "cultural" unfit. It is always best not to criticise the company or its management. Do be generic in your comments and concentrate on the more anonymous "employees" and how they sometimes failed to understand the rationale behind certain decisions.

You could say that because of the size of a company there was sometimes a loss of awareness of the cost of things, hence a loss of understanding of the need for efficiency and economy which only would surface at annual bonus time. Obviously these bonuses are affected by what happens throughout the year and it was a shame that there was not a greater focus on this every day.

Or maybe, you could mention that even though the importance of customer service was emphasized at all time, that sometimes customers were treated as a nuisance and that even though it didn't seem to be the fault of management, it seemed to permeate the company. This made you uncomfortable.

What is your opinion of your last employer?

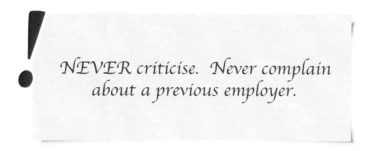

NEVER criticise. Never complain about a previous employer.

One liners are the best "Great", "Very Good", "Excellent" are the right sorts of answers – even if you didn't respect them.

What would you say if I were to tell you that your presentation this afternoon was lousy?

This question is designed to see if you can handle criticism – it is perceives as been a reflection as to whether you are manageable or not. This can be a though question to take if you have been out of work for a while and your self-esteem has taken a knock.

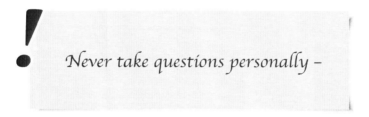

Never take questions personally –

they are all part of the interviewing game. You won't win every game you play – but you don't need to. In the game of employment

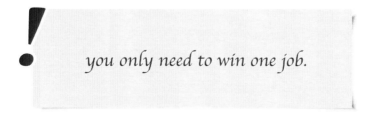

you only need to win one job.

All you need to do is to indicate surprise in your reaction, but remain totally professional.

A good response could be "I'd be surprised, but I'd be eager to find out where you felt I'd gone wrong."

I'm not sure you are suitable for the job.

This could potentially be the last test and another way of saying:" I think that I might like to employ your services, but you need to tell me more about why I should"

This could be an opportunity for you to show your determination, how well you may read things, and of course, your confidence.

Give yourself time to think about which of your strengths and selling points you are going to mention by asking questions.

When you need time – always ask a question.

In this instance you could ask "Why do you say that?"

The interviewer may point out to actual or perceived weaknesses.

Your aim at this stage is to counter by highlighting your strengths, your ability and willingness to learn quickly and continue to develop.

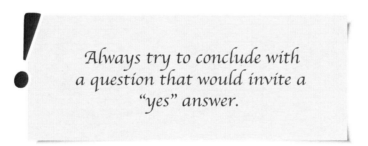

Always try to conclude with a question that would invite a "yes" answer.

You could conclude by saying: "Don't you think that's the real issue?"

Or "Wouldn't you agree?"

Wouldn't you feel better off in another company?

Usually this question is asked only if you are travelling well. If you are making a mess of an interview, the surest sign is that the interviewer will drop back to going through the motions – and try and get the interview concluded as quickly as possible for the sake of both parties!

The best way to handle this one, is to relax, take a deep breath and <u>reverse the play.</u>

"You surprise me. Why would you say that?"

You can buy time, whilst the interviewer is answering you and of course, your answer should be "NO".

Explain why. The interviewer really wants to see that you have done your homework and see how much you know about the company and how determined you are to join it. Showing you have done your research really pays off.

Questions that You Should Not Be Asked, and Don't Have to Answer

These are questions regarding personal matters. Legislation offers protection against discrimination on the grounds of your colour, your sex, your religion, your politics, or your national origin. In some states, and some countries, discrimination on the grounds of age is also illegal.

If you are asked questions that may border on being illegal, it is always best to assume that the interviewer is not fully aware of the legislation in this area.

Here are some examples and suggestions:

How old are you?

You could answer the question in terms of your experience for the position.

Example: "I have had 20 years experience in the banking sector." Then mention your skills as they apply to the job, then ask: "Is age an issue for this position?"

Are you married?

If you are not presently married and perceive it could be an issue, just ask: "Is marital status a condition for this position?"

IN CONCLUSION...

You will definitely stand apart from the average candidate when you know how to successfully debate an interviewer's questions. This will show that you possess negotiation skills which are important in the corporate sector and also contribute to building rapport with them.

Never forget to remain calm,
keep things in perspective,
give as good as you get,
and take it all in good faith.

No one can intimidate you without your permission!

Remember to thank the interviewer for their time and tell them that you enjoyed the interview. Always leave on a positive note.

The Importance of Practice

Always remember how important practice is, by answering your most feared questions into a tape recorder, PC. Ipod, Iphone and then listen to yourself. This will enlarge your arsenal of questions, so that you don't keep asking the same ones and ensuring that your answers are complete and don't leave room for the interviewer to ask you to expand further.

Here are some further examples of typical questions for use in your practice sessions:

- Tell me about yourself.
- What have you done in the way of self-development in the past year?
- What does your partner/spouse think about the possibility of your taking this position?
- Describe a typical day in your present position
- What performance appraisal procedures do you use in evaluating your subordinates?
- Can you work under pressure?
- Under what conditions do you work best?
- What are you looking for in your next job?
- Why should we hire you?
- Have you ever done any public speaking? What feedback did you get?
- How do you define doing a good job?
- Tell me about the best idea you ever sold to your superior.
- Describe the biggest problem you've faced in the past year. How did you handle it?
- How have you benefited from your disappointments?
- Have you ever dismissed an employee?
- How long would you stay with the company?
- What are the limits of your authority in your present job?
- How do you handle stress?
- What are your greatest strengths?
- How long would it take you to make a contribution?
- What interests you most about this job?
- What do you hope to be doing five years from now?
- How do you plan your daily activities?
- Tell me about an experience in your career that really challenged you.
- What have your other jobs taught you?
- How do you see yourself carrying out your responsibilities in this job?
- In what ways has your job prepared you for greater responsibility?
- How good are your listening skills?
- How would your subordinates rate you as a leader? How do you know?
- In what respects do you feel your last boss could have done a better job?
- Tell me about a situation in which your work was criticised.
- What problems do you have in getting along with others?
- What event in your career are you most ashamed of?
- How many hours a week do you find it necessary to work to get your job done?
- How do you provide recognition to subordinates? How well does it work?

- If I were your manager, how would I get the best out of you?
- What are your major motives for working?
- How ambitious are you?

Behavioural Interview

Behavioural Questions

The Behavioural Interview Questions are designed to probe your past behaviour in specific situations, selected for their relevance to critical job events.

Hiring decision often result from adding up the assessments in this area.

The principle of the behavioural interview is based on the principle of best personnel prediction, where the best predictor of future behaviour/performance is past behaviour/performance in SIMILAR CIRCUMSTANCES.

Superlative adjectives (most, last, least, toughest, worst, etc..) are the key to effective behaviour description questions.

First: These questions will help stimulate specific events in your mind which will make it easier for you to respond, WITH AWARENESS.

Secondly: The interviewer will know where the "incident" fits on the scale of all similar incidents.

Thirdly: These questions imply that you did have an experience in this area, as most people do.

What the interviewer is interested in is to hear how you handle a situation, as a predictor of potential future situations with the company you are applying for a position with.

The various areas of experience, or skills, as below, have examples of questions with the aim to define your behaviour in them.

For example, if you tell the interviewer that one of your strength is Strategic Planning, what do you actually mean by that? Can you cite specific examples to support this?

If you claim to have exercised initiative, can you give an example, or describe a situation that illustrates this?

The following titles, cover such categories, and I would urge you to practice them as you will find them tremendously supportive at your interview.

Strategic Planning

Q.   Could you please run me through the processes you go through to put together a strategic plan? Could you give me a specific example of a strategic plan that you have put together successfully in the past?

_____   *What were your specific responsibilities?*

_____   *What was your level of ownership?*

_____   *What was the outcome of the planning exercise?*

_____   *What decision was made?*

_____   *Who made the decision?*

_____   *Who measured the success of the strategic plan?*

Q.   What is one of the most difficult or complex directives you have ever had to implement?

Explain how you approached the task. How successful were you?

Q.   What is one of the most innovative strategies or methods you have used in implementing superior directives? How did you achieve this? How satisfied were you with the end result?

Planning and Organisation

Q.   Can you tell me about a time when you felt you had to juggle a number of tasks to achieve an outcome? What specifically did you do? What was the result?

Q.   Can you describe a working day or week for you? What tools or methods do you use to plan?

Q.   Tell me about a recent situation when you were faced with an excessive workload or competing priorities. What happened? How did you go about organising yourself in that situation? What was the outcome?

Q.   We all have times when we come across unexpected problems which disrupt our plans, describe the last time this happened to you. To what extend had you anticipated that a problem in your plan may occur? How did the problem affect your priorities? What steps did you take to rectify it? What if anything, would you do differently next time to stop this occurring again? Tell me about the day's outcome.

Initiative

Q.   Give me a recent example of when you showed initiative? What were the circumstances? In what way did you show initiative? What resulted from the initiative you took?

Q. Can you outline a suggestion you have made to your supervisor for ways to improve things? How did he/she respond? What was the end result?

Q. Tell me about a time when you referred upwards for help. What was the background? Why did you need help? To what extend do you seek advice in this area?

Q. What changes have you tried to implement in your area of responsibility? What have you done to get them underway? What has been the result?

Q. Describe a situation of when you have had to accept without question what your boss has asked you to do? How did you feel? What happened?

Customer Focus

Q. Describe a situation when you have had to deal with an angry client/customer. What made them angry? What did you do to assist them? How long did this take? What was the outcome?

Q. Tell me about a recent situation when you had to develop a relationship with a new customer. How did you handle this? What was the end result?

Q. Tell me about at time when you were complimented for helping a customer beyond the call of duty. What did you do? How frequently do you go to that kind of trouble? What feedback did you receive?

Q. Can you describe a time when you have had to persuade a customer to rethink their expectations and help them consider alternatives. How did you manage this? What was the outcome?

Ethics and Integrity

Q. Often times we are confronted with the dilemma of having to choose between what is right versus what is best for the company. Can you provide two examples of situations in which you faced this dilemma and how you handled them?

Q. Give me an example of an ethical decision you had to make on the job. What factors did you consider in reaching this decision?

Q. Have you ever had to bend the rules or exaggerate a little bit when trying to make a sale? Can you provide an example?

Q. Tell me about an instance where you had to go against company guidelines or policies in order to get something done.

Q. What ethical qualities do you find most important in an organisation? Why do you find these values important? Give me an example of when you have displayed these values.

Q. Tell me about an instance when an organisation you worked for implemented something you did not agree with. How did this affect your attitude and behaviour?

Results Driven

Q.   Tell me about a situation in which you had to cope with a particularly demanding task. What did you do to ensure you coped? How did you feel? How successful were you?

Q.   Tell me about a time when you were especially motivated? What most strongly motivates you to work hard? How does this show itself? What do you do to maintain your motivation levels? Can you provide an example where this approach helped you through a difficult period?

Q.   Give me an example of when you set yourself an ambitious target. What made it so ambitious? How did it compare with other targets you had set yourself? How well did you do?

Q.   How do you respond to setbacks and obstacles when you are trying to achieve deadlines? Describe a time when you were faced with a setback or obstacle when trying to achieve a deadline? What did you do? What happened?

Q.   When have you given up on a task? Why? How did you feel at the time? How do you feel about it now?

Developing Others

Q.   What have you done to develop the people in your current team?

Q.   Describe a situation where you have been able to develop the performance of an underperforming team member. What did you do? How did they respond? What obstacles did you face? What was the end result?

Q.   What have you done to contribute to the development of a high performer in your team?

Q.   Tell me about a time when you inspired a team member to improve their performance? How did you manage the situation? How successful were you?

Negotiation Skills

Q.   Describe the toughest negotiation you have ever been involved in? What made it particularly tough? What was the outcome?

Q.   Please provide me with an example of when a negotiation did not result in a win/win situation for both parties. Why not? How did you handle it? What was the outcome?

Q.   What has been the most satisfying win/win agreement you have negotiated? How did you create this agreement? What did you learn from this?

Q.   How would you describe your negotiation style? Please provide an example.

Ability to Learn

Q.   Can you tell me what new things you have had to learn in your past job? How did you go about learning them? How long did it take you?

Q.   Can you tell me about something particularly difficult that you have had to learn recently? How did you go about doing this? How successful were you?

Q.   Tell me about a time you had to learn something new in a short time. How did you go about teaching yourself? How successful were you?

Interpersonal Skills / Communication

Q.   Describe the biggest or most demanding group you have had to make a presentation to? How did you prepare for it and present it? How successful were you?

Q.   Could you give me an example of a presentation you have made to senior management or client group? Describe how the information was prepared and presented. What was the outcome? What would you do differently next time?

Q.   Describe how you documented your last project. How did you structure it? How long did it take? What was your involvement specifically? What was the outcome?

Problem Solving

Q.   Please describe a difficult problem you have recently been confronted with at work. How did you handle it? What was the outcome?

Q.   Tell me about at time when you were able to anticipate a problem. How did you know the problem was likely to occur? What did you do? How effective was your action?

Q.   Tell me about at time when you had to identify the key cause of a problem. How did you work out the cause? How did you solve the problem? What lesson did you learn?

Q.   Tell me about a recent situation in which you had to be totally objective when reaching a decision. What were the facts you had to review? How did you weigh the different pieces of information? Looking back, what did you think of your decision? What sort of information did this involve? How did you analyse it? What did you learn from the analysis?

Q.   Give a recent example of when you came up with different solutions to a problem. How did you generate your ideas? What did others think of your ideas? How well did they work in practice?

Analytical Skills

Q.   Describe a complicated problem you have had to address on your job? Describe how you identified or gained a better understanding of the problem? What did you do to solve it? What would you do differently next time?

Q.   Tell me about a time where you had to analyse numerical or financial or technical information. Describe the process you used and how useful the information was.

Q.   Can you describe the thought processes that you work through in order to attack a particular problem? How do you go about analysing a problem and creating a solution? Please provide an example.

Q.   Describe any significant ideas that you have conceived in the past year. How did you know that they were needed and would work? Were they used? How did you contribute to their implementation? How well did they work?

Q.   Describe your most recent task/project. What was your involvement? How did you set about working on the project? What obstacles did you face? What are you most proud of in this situation?

Persuading and Influencing

Q.   Give me a recent example of when you negotiated a successful outcome? What did you negotiate? How did you bring the person around? How did you know they were convinced?

Q.   What are your strengths in terms of influencing people? How often do you find yourself influencing others? Can you outline an example where your strengths in influencing were used to your advantage? What could you do to be more effective at influencing others?

Q.   What are some of the best ideas you ever sold to a superior or peer? What were your approaches? How did they react? How successful were you in influencing others to take this on board?

Q.   Can you tell me about a time you had to approach several individuals for support or cooperation? What was your approach? What was the outcome?

Q.   Tell me about a recent time when you persuaded someone to do something which they were initially reluctant to do? What were their initial objections? What different methods did you use to convince them? What was the outcome?

Building Relationships and Networking

Q.   How do you go about building relationships after an initial meeting? What tools do you use? What is an example of a recent success in this area?

Q.   We all meet people we find difficult to get along with. Tell me about the last time this happened to you. What were the circumstances? Why did you find this person difficult to get along with? Why do you think the person acted in this way? What did you do to try to resolve the situation? What was the outcome?

Q.   Tell me about a recent situation in which you have deliberately built and maintained a relationship with an internal or external contact. Why was this relationship important? How did you build this relationship? How have you maintained the relationship since that time? What benefits has this had to the other person?

Q.   When was the last time you were required to introduce yourself to new business people in a social environment? How did you handle this situation? What difficulties did you face? What was the end result?

Team Player

Q.   Tell me about a time when you have felt you contributed to a successful team project? What was your contribution? What was the outcome?

Q.   Describe a time when you had difficulties working with a team? What happened? What did you learn?

Q.   Give me an example of when you had to support others in a team? Why did they need support? What did you do to support them? How did this change things?

Q.   Can you tell me about a situation where you had to work with a group to get a job done? What was your contribution? Please describe the outcome?

Q.   Tell me about a time when you needed to get team members to work together? What did you do? What would you do differently next time?

Q.   Can you give an example of when you helped other team members achieve their goals at the sacrifice of your own time and effort? How did you manage this? What was the outcome?

Leadership / Management

Q.   What do you do to set an example for your team members? When was the last time you saw a team member emulate your example?

Q.   What happened when you last had to look after a poor performer in your team? How did you initiate the discussions towards solving the issue? What actions did you take to deal with the situation? What was the outcome?

Q.   Please provide examples of how you motivate your team. Please provide examples of when you have put a specific motivator in place to achieve an outcome.

Q.   Can you give me an example of when you have had an outcome to be achieved and you encountered negativity and criticism from your peer group. How did you handle that? What was the result?

Q.   Describe a time when it has been your responsibility to take charge and coordinate a group of people. Tell me about the surrounding circumstances. How did you organise your team? What was your management style? Discuss your objectives and the outcome.

Commercial Acumen

Q.   What can improve the profitability of your present company? Please provide specific examples?

Q.   How do you guide/influence the bottom-line? Please provide a specific answer.

Q.   What are the major threats and opportunities for your business? What have you done to address this?

Q.   What do you do to keep up to date with your own commercial and business knowledge? When was the last time your abilities in this area were of benefit?

Q.   What do you know about your competitors? What do you think they do better than you do? How could you be more successful? What opportunities do you see for more business in this area?

Q.   What is the most important thing you have done to increase profit? What prompted you? What long-term impact did you have? How could you have increased this further?

Q.   Tell me about a time when you have made some cost saving in the past? What did you do? How much money do you think you saved?

Achievement Orientation

Q.   In your recent career, what do you feel is your greatest achievement?

Q.   Can you give me some examples of experiences in your current job that are most satisfying to you? Why are they so satisfying?

Q.   What steps have you taken in the last year to improve your own performance?

Q.   Give me an example of when you worked the hardest and felt the greatest sense of achievement?

Q.   Describe your involvement in a task or project that had to be done with an agreed timeframe and be of an excellent work standard.

Q.   What motivates/de-motivates you about current job? How do you know when you succeed?

Q.   Tell me about a time when you weren't very pleased with your performance. What did you do about it? What was the outcome?

Tenacity

Q.   Describe a situation in which you have given all but failed? How did you react to the outcome? How do others in your team know when you are disappointed with a result?

Q.   Describe your involvement in a task or project that had to be done in a specific timeframe and be of an excellent standard. How did you go about it? What was the outcome?

Q.   Can you relate to an experience in which you felt you persisted too long? How could the situation have been improved?

Q.   What are some of the biggest obstacles you have had to overcome to get where you are today? How did you manage this? To what do you attribute your success?

Q.   Tell me about a time when you thought you weren't going to achieve an expected result? How did you respond? What was the impact?

Q.   Tell me about at time at work where you took on a task/project that made you feel you were out of your depth. How did you tackle this situation? What was the outcome? How did you feel about this situation?

Tolerance for Stress

Q.   What kinds of pressures do you feel in your job? How do you typically deal with pressure?

Q.   What are the highest pressure situations you have experienced in recent years? How did you cope with it? What was the end result?

Q.   Tell me about a time when you have had to deal with a very angry customer? What did you do? What was the outcome?

Q.   What conditions are frustrating you most at...?

Q.   How do you relax or get away from it all (relieve work tensions) after a hard day?

Q.   Tell me about at time when your stress levels impacted your performance? What happened? What did you learn from this situation?

How to Present and Sell Yourself at the Interview

Your Objectives in the Interview

The executive universe has changed with overwhelming speed in the recent years. This necessitates a high level of flexibility which has become an ever more essential attribute for anyone aspiring to be or remain in an executive position. These changes have necessitated flexibility extended to responsibilities, but also to companies or even careers as circumstances demand it.

It is time to take a new approach to presenting and seeling your services. Whether you are seeking to develop your career through "permanent" employment or through contract or consulting work, it is time for a new perspective on your role. As an executive, you are not just a provider of services to an organisation. You are responsible for ensuring those services are appropriately positioned to meet the needs of the market. And you are responsible for **presenting and selling** them.

In short, what you are really doing is running a business. I would strongly suggest that you start looking at your self and your role as being that of the Managing Director of *Myself Company Pty Ltd.*

It this role, you will encounter intense competition. You have to become a polished and effective sales person for your services. When you attend an interview, it's not enough to recognise that you need to be capable o0..f effectively explaining what you can do for the organisation. In the interview, you must accomplish three basic objectives, in fact. These are **to impress, to evaluate and to proceed.**

Your first task it to **impress**. Do not forget that you are in a selling situation.

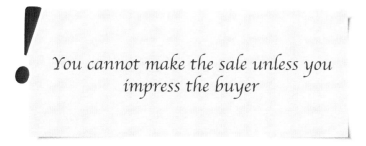

You cannot make the sale unless you impress the buyer

Impress the buyer more favourably than your competition does. At every moment of your contact, your behaviour must be directed toward creating, maintaining or enhancing the right impression.

Your second objective, **evaluation** , because the information you gain in the interview will help you to make a decision as to whether you are interested to work for them, or may provided important benchmark information in assessing another position or offer.

Your third objective is to **proceed.** If your assessment of the organisation and the opportunity available is sufficiently favourable that you want to progress further, the ideal outcome is to be able to do so immediately. Especially in the career transition process,

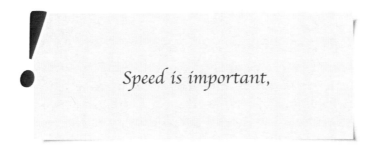

Speed is important,

as an impressive new candidate may come onto the scene, a hiring freeze may be imposed or you may simply be forgotten as other candidates are more successful than you in attracting or retaining the interviewer's favourable attention.

Of course, you're not in the driver's seat in regard to the timing of the hiring decision. The timing of that decision is always the buyer's prerogative. But there are often things you can do to influence the timing. And even it if can't be influenced, it's vital that you understand the timing of the decision. That knowledge will put you in a better position to influence the decision itself.

Creating the Right Impression

Creating the right impression will involve you demonstrating, that you are **willing** to do the job, that you are **able** to do it, and that you are **manageable.** When you go into the interview, it should be with a clear strategy for doing so in each case.

Your **willingness** can be readily demonstrated by your projection, throughout the interview, of enthusiasm. Use it to energise the discussion. High levels of enthusiasm create vivid impressions – the kind you want to leave. This must of course, be handled with skill and subtlety.

To demonstrate **ability**, it's not enough to possess the skills required for the job. You must be able to **impart confidence that you do possess those skills** and are comfortable in using them. This is why it is important to practice your skills in presenting and selling yourself, to your partner, friend, friends, colleagues, etc for you to develop confidence in your presentation.

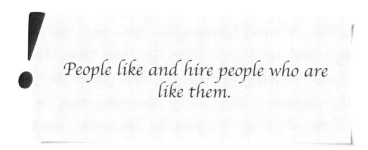

People like and hire people who are like them.

To demonstrate manageability, you must convey that you LIKE the interviewer. Because we all tend to believe that we are reasonable people, we naturally believe that those who like us will be cooperative and easy to work with.

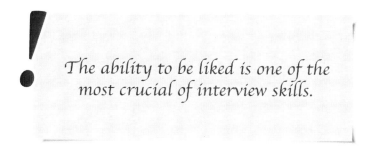

The ability to be liked is one of the most crucial of interview skills.

You must demonstrate that you possess a sufficiently flexible range of behaviours that on one hand you can get the job done, whatever the opposition, while on the other hand, you possess the sensitivity to the needs of superiors that is required to function in a way that is supportive of them .

You will find these points important to keep in min:

- The first four minutes are crucial
- Don't "pretend" to win a position or you will deceive yourself and your future employer
- **Prepare** for specific characteristics and achievements you want to convey such as energy, motivation, confidence, dedication, financial improvements or cost reductions achieved, and efficiency. **Practice** them – and how you will present them and illustrate them.
- Rehearse answers to the kinds of questions you think you are most likely to be asked. Create opportunities for **role plays**.

Dress for Success

The standard of your dress says much about your self-image, and your level of awareness in general.

During the first four minutes of the interview, in particular, the employer is making a series of quick judgements that will rapidly harden into an overall impression. Once that overall impression has been established, it's not likely to change. Like it or not, our appearance is one of the easier things for others to evaluate about us. So why not make it work for you?

Look around and really OBSERVE the dress standards of today, at executive levels. Recognise that your appearance must be impeccable. The interviewer EXPECTS you to be trying hard. Look the part. But remember to adjust according to the best standards of the organisation concerned.

In general, conservative and traditional is the safest. Quality, style and colour are all vitally important. Watch the television news, ABC for example is usually quite traditional. Note how the presenters are dressed, and use this as your point of reference.

Trust your common sense. Standards vary from one industry to another and from one city and climatic zone to another. However, quality clothing and accessories will always provide an advantage. Here are some guidelines

Guidelines for Men's Clothing:
- Wear a conservative, dark suit. Navy is still best: dark grey is good.
- Shirts should be long-sleeved. White or pale blue shirts are safest, thin stripes are all right.
- Wear a quality tie. Generally, this should be of silk. Appropriate width and colour are important.
- Shoes should be conservative; generally, black is best.
- Accessories must be appropriate. The watch is likely to be unfavourably noticed if it is below the standard of that worn by others at the level of the position for which you are applying.
- A briefcase or folder may be brought to the interview. Generally, this should be of brown or black leather, in the best quality you can afford.

Guidelines for Women's Clothing:
- Whilst women have more latitude in regard to dress than men, the most important point to remember is that to be taken seriously, you must dress like a serious business person.
- A suit is generally essential: acceptable colours are similar to those for men.
- The blouse can be in a wider range of colours than those for men, and may include grey, cream and pale pastels. The best materials are cotton and silk.
- Shoes should be conservative, with low heels or flats.
- Stockings should generally be neutral.
- Jewellery should be conservative.
- Makeup should be subtle.
- A purse, briefcase or folder is acceptable – but only one.

The golden rule for both sexes is – NOTHING OSTENTATIOUS.

The Interview

Here are some general points and principles to keep in mind:

- Your attitude is most important. Your mental state will always shine through. Think of yourself as the Director of our own experience of the interview. You must choose to approach it having the expectation that it will be a fruitful experience! It could even be quite exciting!
- All of us can function at a variety of levels, the two most basic ones, been internal and external: Your internal presentation must be **positive** and your physiology must be at its most potent.

- Support yourself by arriving early and relaxed. Plan your schedule to allow more than enough time in order to cover for any contingencies such as traffic jams, parking hassles, train delays etc.
- You could prepare yourself beforehand with basic relaxation techniques, to maintain a sense of inner calm. Whilst waiting, review your resume and slowly read it. Focus on your strengths and what you will bring to this job and this employer.

Other important points you will find useful:

- Use the interviewer's name early in the interview; to be sure it's cemented in your mind.
- Never criticise a former employer.
- Ask the interviewer if it is ok for you to use their first name.
- Make sure you understand a question before you answer it.
- Never apologise for anything – unless you arrive late (which should never happen).
- Do not crack jokes.
- Use pauses and silences during the interview to your advantage and see them as a chance to collect your thoughts before answering, rather than rushing in to answer before you are ready.
- Never give ANY negative information about yourself – whether personal or career-related.

Let us have a look at the **ECMS** approach to presenting and selling yourself. It will be based on your having something to GIVE an employer, and on INTEGRITY. It will give you an unbeatable edge in pursing any job for which you're qualified.

First of all, you must recognise that you are SELLING something – what you can do for an employer. You must start thinking like a sales person, after all there is a lot of money involved and you must play the game in order to win. It might require a shift in your thinking, but you might as well start now and accept that in today's economy, EVERYONE has to learn how to sell. Since the stakes are high, you might as well learn to think like a TOP salesperson, which involves learning to consciously use techniques for developing rapport, then confidence, and finally for leading.

The start of the interview is the easiest part, all you have to do is to smile, be friendly, and to follow the interviewer's lead.

Let the interviewer set the tone and follow suit.

The second step is to establish rapport and to reassure that you are not a threat.

> **!** *Remember, people like and hire people who are like them.*
> *You must convey that you are LIKE the interviewer*

Once a reasonable level of rapport has been established, you can begin to work on creating confidence as well. You're asking the interviewer to place a great deal of trust in you and you must deserve and be able to win that trust!

You can then slowly begin to employ your selling skills.

Selling does involve human emotions and enthusiasm is essential to succeed in selling. Now that you have established rapport, your own enthusiasm will add to your confidence and belief in yourself, which can be transferred to the interviewer. Of course, you must match your level of enthusiasm to the personality of the interviewer and the level of rapport you've developed.

What the interview is, is a short time frame that you are given to put your case forward. It will take 40 minutes to an hour at the most and you must make the most effective possible use of that time to impart to the interviewer everything you want them to know about yourself. Just imagine an interview that you are watching an interview on TV and how much information is passed on through both parties.

It is important to remember achieving closure in your responses, so that there is no further need for the interviewer to ask anything further on a particular subject.

The Non-Verbal Interview

The importance of practice and rehearsal BEFOREHAND cannot be emphasized enough, because body language never lies.

You will be too busy during the interview to think about how you project yourself, which is why it is important to practice and even ask someone close to you some feed back about it.

There are some simple rules that are good to remember: steady eye contact is considered desirable by most people, but do not stare, and simply match the behaviour of the person you are talking to.

Mirroring is the non-verbal way to be like the interviewer. It's an essential element in establishing rapport and developing confidence. Used properly, it's of great value, but do not overdo it.

LEADING on a non-verbal level is a more advanced technique and involves gradually shifting from mirroring the other person's body language to influencing it, for instance by changing the pace of a bodily movement, so that the other person begins to follow your lead.

The Verbal Interview

What you say in the interview is obviously of great importance, but if there's one other basic point to keep in mind in regard to the verbal portion of the interview, it's this:

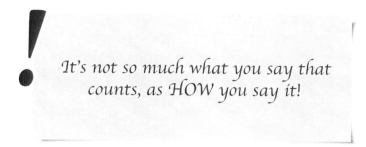

It's not so much what you say that counts, as HOW you say it!

Remain aware of the interviewer's objectives which is to assess you, so help him or her with this assessment through active listening, concise responses, etc. If you are faced with a weak interviewer, you might offer to help and ask such things as : "Would it be helpful if I reviewed....?" (Some area that you'd like to cover, but that the interviewer has neglected to raise).

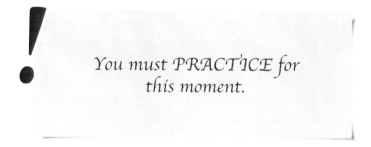

Whilst giving the interviewer assistance in accomplishing his or her objectives, you must be certain that your own objectives are also met.

Your objectives also include that of achieving progress in the hiring process.

None of what you're seeking to accomplish can be expected to just happen

You must PRACTICE for this moment.

It's essential to research the position and prepare yourself with relevant selling points, and to rehearse answers to the most likely questions, as well as those that are likely to derail you.

Use the responses you've planned and rehearsed. Remember to use questions as offering opportunities to direct the conversation along lines favourable to you.

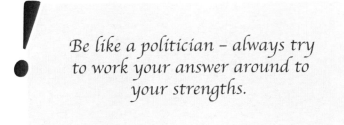

Be like a politician – always try to work your answer around to your strengths.

After all, this is what you have to sell to the employer.

The Importance of Evaluation

Evaluation of course is very much mutual. In today's market, even though the employer is in the dominant position, the candidate still has a pretty good hand to play!

Remain aware and confident that you have a legitimate need to know the answers to many questions. Any experienced interviewer will want to be sure that you have an opportunity to ask them. It is also both strategically and tactically unwise to be too keen to take a position without obtaining satisfactory answers to some important questions. Not getting sufficient information can mean an unsatisfactory move and a short term position that may diminish your future marketability

Make sure that you ask relevant questions, such as:

- Is there someone in this position at present? Why has the position become available?
- Could you tell me about the history of this position? Has there been much turnover in the position? (If so, why?)
- Do you have a written job description for this position? May I see it? (If you haven't had access to it prior to the interview)
- There are a number of characteristics in the advertisement (or the job description) for this position. Could you tell me which you do consider the most important ones?
- Which issues would I be expected to focus on in the first six months?
- What are the most important relationships for successful performance in this position? Are there likely to be any unusual challenges with any of these?
- How will my performance be measured?
- How would success in this position translate in terms of my career prospects?

Interviewers

You will find that most interviewers, especially the executive of the company seeking to fill the position, are not comfortable with the interview process and they usually are untrained or inexperienced interviewers. They usually are aware of their lack of skills in that area and most of the time, are as anxious to please you, as you are to please them!

This presents a wonderful opportunity to capitalise on the magnificent employment opportunity that the incompetent interviewer represents! Have you ever come away from an interview with a head full of information about the company doing the interviewing while the interviewer sits alone in his or her office with no real idea of your management or other skills and their applicability to his or her needs? So here are a few tips to take advantage of this situation:

If the interviewer gets involved into a lengthy discussion about the company or the position...

This is the inexperienced interviewer's most frequent shortcoming and you can maximise the benefit to you:

- Make sure that you look REALLY interested, sit up straight on the edge of your chair, nod at the appropriate times and encourage the information delivery with comments such as: "Sounds tremendous," "Really?" "Great".
- Finally, as soon as there is a pause, take control.
- Do thank the interviewer for taking the time to explain these things. Tell them it has given you a real feel for the position and company and it has given you the chance to see how well the position fits your experience and abilities (list these).
- Then ask the interviewer to tell you of any other job requirements outside the abilities that you have listed.
- If there are further requirements mentioned, seize the chance to show precisely how your background fits you for these too. You could ask "Would it be of value, Mr Jones, if I outlined my experience in that area with XYX Company?"

If the interviewer is unprepared, their desk is a mess and your cv is buried amongst others or the interviewer has just begun to speedily re-read it...

- Unfortunately, this is not unusual, and the best way to handle this is to remain totally quiet and calm because it is the interviewer who is under pressure now. Just breathe deeply, remain composed and give yourself the advantage of calmness.
- Under these circumstances, the more relaxed and composed you are, the more the interviewer will absorb that mood, the less hassled he or she feels, the more he or she will like you. You can turn this to your advantage.

If the interviewer spends time telling you about the culture of the company

- Immediately relate to what is being said.
- Tell them that you have always wanted to work in such an environment and that you really think it brings the best out in people including you.

If the interviewer talks about negative elements of the position and almost seems to be trying to put you off...

- This could be a position that they might have had difficulty filling or have had the wrong sort of person in the position historically.
- Tell the interviewer your greatest strengths and how you believe they will enable you to do the job.

- Ask them to tell you what some of the biggest problems in the job are.
- Outline elements from your background to show that you will be able to more than handle these.

If the interviewer only seems to ask questions that invite one word answers...

- Answer as invited, then push on and expand on the answer ."That's an excellent point Mr Jones. I couldn't agree more. When I was at XYZ Company that is something I learned a lot about..."

If the interviewer asks a stream of stress questions...

You would be surprised how much it can make the interviewer feel just as uncomfortable as they believe it makes you! Remember that people like to be liked. Your interviewer is probably no exception but they may have specific criteria's that need to be answered as part of their interviewing policies.

- Don't take such questions personally. This is just part of some of their procedures, just keep your composure.

Remember this principle: First impressions are the most important! Once you have weathered the first four minutes of an interview and got things shaded in your favour, the rest is relatively plain sailing. Messing up a question later in the interview is rarely as disastrous as getting off to a poor start.

Difficult Interview Situations

Certain interview situations tend to cause people particular distress, and you might find these suggestions helpful:

- The stress interview, group selection processes or panel interviews. Remember, if you can handle it in real life, you can handle it in an interview.
- Over a meal. Eat little; eat simply. Avoid alcohol or if this is difficult drink only one glass.
- In public places. This can be used to advantage. Get there first. Be able to lead the way to a quiet corner.
- Psychological tests. Get used to the idea that you may have to cope with sitting down and completing a "psych test" before you are appointed to an executive position. In one sentence, the basic rule for handling these is: Answer questions in these sorts of tests from the point of view of your highest professional aspirations, such as your best professional self. The best way to prepare for these is a positive attitude, and arriving adequately rested.

Closing the Interview

You must find out where things are headed from here. So you must ask and state the following:

- Are there to be subsequent interviews? With whom? WHEN? If the information is not volunteered, you must ask it.
- Close. You must repeat that you believe that you can do a good job for the employer and wish to make it clear that you would like the opportunity to do so.
- If offered the job, don't look to anxious to take it, if at all possible, sleep on it, and request to call them first thing the following morning to confirm your acceptance.
- Avoid the following:
- Don't discuss salary or benefits if you can avoid it – unless you've received an offer. If you are made an offer, you must have a figure in mind to negotiate from or discuss.
- Don't press for an early decision. Timing is the interviewer's prerogative.

What You Need to Do after the Interview

You will find helpful to do the following:

1. Complete an "Interview Debrief" form as soon as possible after the interview. Don't wait until you get home or back to work – your impressions of the interview must be totally fresh.
2. As soon as possible after the interview, send an email to the interviewer! This must be done to cement the favourable impression you have created during the interview. Be sure to review the material on follow up letters and the sample letters provided. You can choose to send an email or a formal letter, although, these days, emails are the accepted form of communication and of course, it is instantly received.
3. If you haven't heard anything after five working days (unless you were advised that a longer time frame would be involved) – pick up the phone and when speaking to the interviewer, do repeat the points made in your letter, repeat that you would like the job, and finish with this question

   "Mr Jones, I am totally confident that I can fulfil all the requirements of the position. I am really keen on securing this role. Could you please tell me what I have to do to get it?

   Then shut up and wait for the answer.

In Case of Rejection

You must look upon it as a temporary setback. You must also forget your ego. Thousands will be rejected this week. That is not an issue. The best candidate for any job does not always get it.

> *The best prepared and most determined is the one who gets the position!*

ECMS is the system that will get you "best prepared" but only you can do the "most determined" part!

Don't Take "No" as a Rejection

When our children ask us for something, we often say no. When they persist, we may still say no. However, how often are they able to change that apparent rejection into a yes? The same principle applies to any other action we take throughout life.

If our mindset is one of determination to achieve "something", we will invariably achieve it.

NO does not always mean no. It can mean:

- "Not now, I'm busy"
- "I've had a bad day"

Or in the case of an employer...

- "I'm under pressure to hire someone else"
- "I can't pay that much"
- "I don't want to make a decision"
- "Tomorrow would be a better time to talk about it"
- "I don't have enough information"
- "I'm not sold yet"
- "I need more skills in a different area" etc.

You must realise once and for all, that NO does not equate to a rejection of you and all you stand for! It is a reflection of the person who said it and the conditions at that time. It has nothing to do with your competence, your worthiness, or our desirability as an employee. If does not mean that you are not likeable or that you are not employable. The next section explains more about the reasons this could occur.

What to Do When You Have Been Rejected

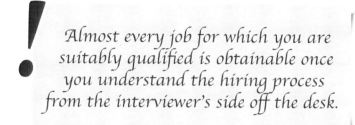

Almost every job for which you are suitably qualified is obtainable once you understand the hiring process from the interviewer's side off the desk.

If you are rejected after the interview, the reason why usually comes down to one of these reasons:

1. The interviewer does not think you can do the job
2. He/she does not feel your profile fits the needs of the position
3. He/she did not like you
4. He/she did not feel your personality would fit the position and the corporate culture

I don't need to tell you that failure is often due to quitting just before success. The same principle applies here, with you not quitting. Pick up the phone, talk to the hiring executive, and discuss the matter further. Ask for the reason for the rejection. Express understanding of the reason given, and if the situation permits, offer a valid reason for reconsideration of the situation (for example, interview nerves during the first interview), express enthusiasm, and ask for another interview. Determination can sway their final decision and give you another chance to meet and to stand out. And at your next interview - sell yourself again and close again!

In adopting this attitude, you prove yourself to be a fighter – a quality universally respected and admired. Your interviewer will want to see you succeed because you are made of the right stuff. You have shown guts, tenacity and drive – the hallmark of a winner.

Of course, it may well be too late for this particular job – but you will enhance the interviewer's opinion of you. And the interviewer may well know of future planned vacancies where you can now start as a favourite. Don't forget that in most companies these days, hiring and firing responsibilities are typically spread across a number of managers – a vacancy brought to your attention in another division with a positive endorsement from your interviewer may be a recipe for success. Remember to say to the interviewer that you would like to work for the company/group of companies and to ask if there is anyone else they know of to whom you should be talking. Make every post a winning post. Quite apart from anything else, this is good positive reinforcement for you and your program.

Remember, the world still tends to make way for those who know where they're going!

Accessing the Hidden Market

The employment hiring statistics of the past 25 years show that 8% of management vacancies in advanced countries such as the U.S., U.K., Canada and Australia have been filled without advertising, either by the employer or by a recruitment consultant on the employer's behalf. A study by the American Sociological Association was released on the 7th August 2009 stipulating that 9.6% positions in the states were filled without advertising.

In support of this, the ABS (Australian Bureau of Statistics) figures reveal an even higher percentage. In fact the ABS released figures that are closer to 77- 82% of vacancies for managers, administrators and professionals are never advertised. And for other categories of employee, the figure for non-advertised positions is higher still!

There are major reasons that so few positions are advertised.

- A major issue in executive hiring decisions is confidentiality. Once a position is advertised, this is difficult to maintain, even if a search firm is working to fill the role.
- Another important consideration is cost. Even if an employer hires without using an executive recruitment consultant, advertising a position is expensive – and could cost from $2,000 to $15,000 . If a consultant's services are used, these costs can rise spectacularly. Typically, placement fees at management level are between 18% to 30% of the salary package – including the value of company car, superannuation etc. And advertising costs are added to this amount. If a "head hunter" is hired, the costs are far higher still.
- There is an additional factor, with is time, as the processing of applications in response to an advertisement is very time-consuming.
- The risk factor of hiring through advertising is much higher than employing someone referred by others or known to the employer. When the candidate or the person providing the referral is well known to the employer, this can provide a high level of reassurance regarding the rightness of the hiring decision.
- Many positions are of course filled internally, without the need for consideration of outside candidates.

There is an additional avenue of employment, which is more limited, through Executive Search firms, and more importantly through networking and the various forms of direct contact are the sole means of tapping the "hidden market".

This section of **ECMS** covers the techniques of accessing this "hidden market".

It is so important to recognise the extraordinary enormity of the opportunity available to those who are aware of the techniques of accessing this rich source of job opportunities. Very few people handle this area of career management well. Those who do so, enjoy a major advantage.

Networking is the most effective means of accessing the hidden market. Its principles are easy to master and must be embraced by those "between jobs".

It is vital that those in certain other categories also make networking the centre piece of their career search strategy:

- If you are over 50, it is a fact of life that it is generally more difficult for more mature job seekers to make a change through the advertised market.
- If you are making a career change. The specification provided by a company to a recruitment consultant, defining the characteristics and experience of the person sought, will normally specify a track record for a minimum period in a particular industry or in a similar role. If you're making a fairly significant change in direction it's unlikely you will meet these criteria.
- If you are uncertain of your future direction. Networking is an information gathering exercise and, as you meet and receive feedback from increasing numbers of people, your ideas will crystallise and you will see with greater clarity the type of role that really suits you. Importantly, you will also learn about the employers in this niche market thus making it easier to target them.

If you are currently employed, but you are seeking a change to a similar but more challenging role, networking is also definitely recommended. Obviously, you must be aware that unless your networking is performed on a very confidential basis, there is always a risk that your effort to seek a career change could become known to your employer. Nonetheless, your motivation to expand your career and improve yourself in most cases is very unlikely to lead to your involuntary and premature departure from your employer.

You will find that the energy generated through networking will give you a greater purpose to life, especially if you are between jobs. You have appointments to arrange, companies to research, visits to make and thank you letters to write. Instead of waiting helplessly for a letter or phone call after you have responded to an advertisement or for a phone call after an interview, you'll have much to do in planning your networking. Not only is this mentally stimulating and helpful in regard to morale but career search is a numbers game and the more people you see and companies you visit, the sooner you are likely to get the job you want.

Approaching the Market

Your first task in networking is to write a list of all the people you know. Start with your relatives and friends and then work on covering professional people with whom you have recently dealt, such as your accountant, financial planning adviser, auditors, stock broker, lawyer, insurance agent, doctor, dentist, real estate agents etc. Then think of people you have met in the course of work – suppliers, customers, auditors, consultants, competitors, public relations and advertising agency personnel, contacts you made at trade association meetings, seminars, course, Institute of Management functions, Chamber of Commerce meetings, clubs (both sporting and social) etc. Then consider retirees, people on the move, community organisation officers, Government agency officers, Parent-Teacher Association officers and members, acquaintances in religious organisation, small business owners, outplacement class associates etc. Once you have started you will find the list grows as more names come to mind over the following next few days. Are you aware that the average adult knows from four hundred to seven hundred people!

Consultants are a particularly rich source of contacts, for example, those with whom you may have worked in installing programs such as JIT, TQM, MRPII, Business Process Re-engineering, Benchmarking, new software etc.

Do join those organisations which represent you or similar ones and do make a point of attending those functions where you think there will be opportunities for meeting people.

Your goals as a networker are quite straightforward

- As you gather information about industry or professional trends, problems and needs, you will be able to more accurately define your target market and you will come to understand where you might be able to provide solutions to those problems and needs.
- Networking is a powerful tool to employ additional "eyes and ears" in your career search. By bringing your contacts into your search for new employment, you are less likely to miss opportunities that are never advertised or listed with recruiters.
- Always keep your main objective in mind when networking and that is to get even more referrals from your contacts and meet even more people who will give you valuable insights and keep an eye open for you. In fact, you will know you are networking correctly when you begin meeting new contacts who were previously strangers. Indeed networking is not just meeting those people you know, but most importantly generating new contacts. This is the only way to enlarge your circle of associates.

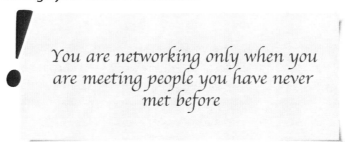

There is a huge benefit in networking; there are no hidden agendas. You are simply trying to get help, information and names from the people with whom you arrange meetings.

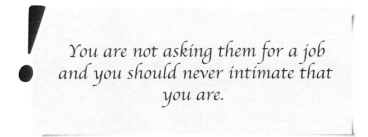

You are not asking them for a job and you should never intimate that you are.

Information, help and names are what you want from your contacts and that's all you should expect.

Never rule out visiting somebody whose role is markedly different from your field of endeavour. If you're an accountant and somebody suggests visiting a nuclear physicist, go ahead and arrange the meeting. The fact that they are working in nuclear physics doesn't preclude their knowing people, either in their business network or in their social network, who could be in the same industry or in a similar position as you.

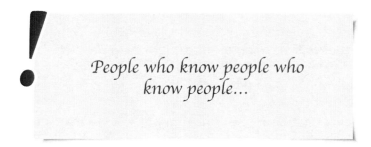

People who know people who know people...

Usually, you will find that if you are recommended to contact a person in an industry far different from yours, he or she will turn out be very gregarious and a rich source of referrals.

Objectives

Now that you have completed your list, you should start telephoning each person to arrange a meeting. We suggest you request a twenty-minute meeting. You will find that in reality, networking meetings average some forty minutes. Your objectives at each meeting should be as follows:

- To meet your contact, show them your resume and obtain their thoughts on industry trends, issues, prospects, your future career direction, people to contact and companies to which they think your particular skills and achievements are suited.
- To enter their network so that, after reading your resume and talking with you, they will have a clear understanding of your achievements and capabilities. You never know who your contact will meet tomorrow at the golf club or a business lunch who is looking for a person such as you for either a project or on a permanent basis!
- Your aim is to obtain referrals. You should aim to gain at least two leads from each meeting so your network continually grows.

Telephone Techniques

It is highly recommended that you give careful thought to the approach you are going to take on the phone with each person and rehearse it so that it comes over confidently. Your phone call should be along the following lines:

> *"Hello, Peter. This is John Smith. I'm currently exploring career opportunities <u>and feel sure you can help me</u>. I would very much appreciate it if you could spare me twenty minutes at your office. I would like to show you my brief resume <u>and I am sure you that would be able to suggest</u> a couple of people to contact and a few companies to think about. I would also welcome the opportunity to discuss industry trends, issues and prospects."*

There are two particularly important passages in the above. The first is the phrase "I feel sure you can help". This is a compliment, which everybody enjoys. It is also an unmistakable request for help. Remarkably few people reject a straightforward request for help, especially when complimented, no matter how busy or senior they are.

The second key passage is the one in which you make it clear that you would like your contact to read your resume (Your brief resume) and discuss people and companies to visit. It is good to have at least 2 versions of your resume and in this instance a brief version to give to your future networking executive to read. This shows that you <u>are not asking them for a job</u> and, accordingly, they are not placed on the defensive or likely to become ill at ease.

Obviously the content of the phone call will be varied if you don't know the person particularly well or if it is some time since you last met. In such cases be ready after you've said "I'm exploring career opportunities and feel sure you'll be able to help me" to briefly outline the key features of your career and particularly the title of your current or most recent position. All you need do is to give a very brief summary, so your contact can position you in his or her mind.

An alternative approach, which we recommend when you don't know the person well, or don't know the person at all, is to say that <u>you are contemplating an industry move</u>. Whilst you have already done a considerable amount of research you feel it would be invaluable to have the opportunity of discussing their views on the industry, its trends, problems and opportunities, companies on the way down or the way up, the state of the job market, salary levels etc.

In such cases your phone call would be something like this:

> *"Hello, John. This is Paul Jones. I am currently between jobs following a corporate re-structure. I have given much thought and conducted some research into the possibilities of moving into the health industry. With your experience, I believe you would really be able to help me and I wondered if you could spare me twenty minutes to discuss the challenges and opportunities in your industry. I'll bring my brief cv and if you could glance through it I'm sure you would be able to tell me about the opportunities for somebody with my career history and achievements. I believe you would also be the ideal person to suggest other people in the industry to give me further insights".*

The average duration of your phone call should be about three minutes.

A Few Tips

- **Do** practice and rehearse your telephone script. You must sound confident and fluent.
- **Do** start with your first "cold" referrals, those people you have never met before and call them one after the other. Don't worry if your words don't flow easily and confidently with the first one or two. You'll be fine by the fourth or fifth.
- **Do** introduce yourself clearly.
- **Do** smile when you speak. It puts warmth into your conversation.
- **Do** ask your contacts for a "very brief meeting", or to "share a cup of coffee" with you.
- **Don't** read your telephone script. If you read it, it will sound as though you are reading it, even if you have rehearsed !
- **Do not** apologise, like "I'm sorry to bother you". This puts your contact in command of the situation and you will end up on the defensive.
- Do not refer to the possibility of vacancies – "I know you don't have any vacancies but ..." this puts the pressure on that person, by implying you're really after a job in their organization. This will put them on the defensive and it also sounds depressing.
- **Do not** use the word "interview" at all. This immediately implies that you are seeking a job interview.
- **Do not** waste time on initial small talk. The first impression is crucial. Your contact is likely to be busy and their time is precious to them.
- **Do not** talk too much. You must keep the target's attention and get them contributing. Say what you have to say, then shut up and listen and your <u>aim is not to have a conversation over the telephone, but to set a time to meet with them</u>.
- **Don't** be slow or incomplete when answering questions.
- **Do** listen! Give your contact time to talk.
- **Don't** feel you are exploiting people. Remember that most people want to help and give advice. They like to be treated as experts and give their opinions.
  You have to ask to receive.

- **Do not** overstay your welcome. Once a meeting is set up, thank the person and get off the phone immediately.

Script Example: Setting Up a Meeting with a Colleague

Hello John, this is Peter Jones. You may recall we met at the ABC meeting recently.

General chat and how are you.

The reason for my call John, is to ask for your assistance with some information.

I'm researching several industries to ascertain potential growth and trends and so I can see where I can make a contribution using my skills.

I was impressed with what you had to say when we met, and I would appreciate the opportunity to meet with you for about twenty minutes to discuss a couple of issues and get some information from your perspective. Is that OK with you?

Great, how are you placed in the next week or so? *(Suggest two times if this will help to secure the meeting and end on a decisive note.)*

Script Example: Setting Up a Meeting with a Referral

Hello Peter. My name is *John Barnes* and I have been given your name by a mutual colleague of ours _____.

I'm researching several industries to assist me in planning my career.

Paul suggested that as the *CEO* of your organisation, you are the best person to give me the particular information I am seeking, specifically regarding your industry's growth potential and emerging trends.

I'd like the opportunity to meet with you for twenty minutes to discuss these issues. I'm happy to meet late afternoon or early morning if that would be more convenient for you. How are you placed in the next week or so?

Gate Keepers

Successful networking depends on bypassing receptionists and personal assistants. Your heartfelt request for help is unlikely to gain a spontaneous "yes" if conveyed by a personal assistant along the lines of

> *"There's a Mr .... on the line and he wants to meet you so you can help him find a job".*

The best time for phoning is in the hour from 8.00 to 9.00am, before the personal assistant arrives for work, which will usually be at the start of normal office hours even if your target executive comes in an hour early. Similarly, after 5:30pm is a reasonably good time, although if your referral had a particularly difficult day, the reception of your call may not be as positive.

> *First thing in the morning is best.*

If the receptionist wants to put you through John Smith's personal assistant, you would sound confident and authoritative by saying "This is Peter Jackson, for John Smith". This will make it seem suggestive of pre-existing friendship.

It is wise to make personal assistants your allies rather than seek to avoid them and thereby antagonise them.

They will invariably say the Mr Smith is unavailable at present. I'm his executive assistant. Can I help?

Your response is critical: Certainly, I'd be grateful for your assistance. I'm trying to set up a meeting with Mr Smith and I realise he's a very busy man. I wonder if you could suggest a time for an appointment, or perhaps a time when I could phone back and talk to him.

Once involved with personal assistants, this answer creates a dependence on them, which may be of great value if you need to ring back two or three times. It is wise to keep them involved rather than cut them out and risk upsetting them. Always make a note of their names. Apart from the elementary courtesies it will help in gaining their whole-hearted cooperation if you address them personally.

It is likely that the secretary will subject you to some further screening before putting you through to the executive concerned or assisting you in establishing a meeting. We suggest you say that you are researching career opportunities, and wish to discuss this with the executive, as they are well known in the ABC industry. Obviously, you must state the same reason for the meeting when you speak to the executive. They will not be happy if they feel you have tricked their personal assistant into letting the call through.

If at all possible, it is better not to leave a message for your referral to call you back. If they call back, they have control over the conversation, and will probably want to know who you are, what you want, they might be on the defensive and might think that you want to sell them something. Also, if they are ringing you, they have the initiative and might catch you unprepared, which is not the best environment for you to obtain their agreement to a meeting.

Potential Challenges

Once you have made contact with the person with whom you wish to arrange a meeting, try to avoid putting them in a position where they start to say "Why don't you put your resume in the mail and I'll get back to you with my thoughts". This would mean the end of the road for that line of networking. The chances are that your contact won't get back to you so there's no opportunity to obtain at least two referrals. Also, this means that you will fail to see your contact in their office and discuss your resume and your future, so that you never have the chance to enter their network.

Equally, if it is suggested that you send your resume to their Human Resources Manager, It would also mean the end of the road for any line of networking with that particular contact. Human Resources Managers have been trained over the years to save management from time-consuming unsolicited job seekers. It is also relevant and important for you to remember that Human Resource Managers are not the decision makers when it comes to hiring personnel. The decisions are made by the Managing Director, General Manager or Divisional Management depending on the nature of the job and the size of the organization.

Usually you will be able to spot the times when somebody is about to say: "Why don't you send your resume in?"

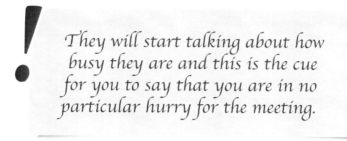

They will start talking about how busy they are and this is the cue for you to say that you are in no particular hurry for the meeting.

Tell your prospect that you are happy to meet in a few week's time and at any time which is convenient, perhaps at 7.00p.m., and maybe even at 7.30a.m., or at lunch or over a coffee.

Regarding HR People

We advise against networking with Human Resources personnel if your real objective is to establish a networking meeting with a key decision maker in a particular company. However, remember that Human Resources personnel frequently have very large networks themselves, because they move around companies but tend to stay in the same profession. You will find them particularly helpful in networking – **as providers of leads** – except insofar as their own companies are concerned. They can also be excellent at being another set of "eyes and ears" for you.

Whilst the mechanics of networking are simple, don't be put off because the networking pathways can take various twists and turns. Indeed, to the uninitiated, they seem based on luck. The payoff seems vague, elusive and uncontrollable. For these reasons many executives fail to accept networking as the highly efficient self-marketing method it is and the MOST EFFECTIVE METHOD of penetrating that almost 80% of the market which is not advertised.

Annual Seek Survey

According to SEEK's *Employee Satisfaction and Motivation Survey*, in November 2009, a growing number of candidates are going directly to corporate career sites or *using their personal networks to source jobs*. The annual SEEK survey of more than 6,000 employees and job seekers found that 36% believed they would get their next job directly through a recruitment company, down from 40% a year earlier, and 43% in 2007.

However, some 88% said they expected to get their next job through a job board (the ads on which are largely posted by recruitment companies).

Some 38% of candidates said they expected to find a new role by *networking with family and friends*, up by 3 percentage points - suggesting that using personal networks is now seen as an increasingly viable method of finding a job.

Using specific company websites also grew in popularity, up 3 percentage points to 32%, and making a direct approach to the organisation was stable at 33%.

Just 11% of candidates said they were likely to find a job through social networking websites.

More Advice

Networking and introducing yourself to an unknown market, equates branding yourself, which means making choices about who you want to be known as, about how you wish to be perceived in the market.

None of us can be all things to all people.

DO NOT say "I'm a business generalist - I can work in any function, and manage any situation."

You need to introduce yourself in a way that helps new contacts understand and retain

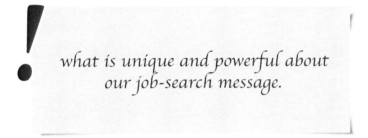

what is unique and powerful about our job-search message.

That means, forgoing the two-hour explanation of every job we've ever held, and zeroing in on a powerful message that a new friend can carry forward for us.

It could be something like this: "I have developed and launched 15 consumer products, in 16 chain stores, that generated at least $70M in revenue in their first year on the market." THAT is good and powerful and memorable.

Another example: "I am an HR manager with a specialisation in recruiting; at XYZ company, I filled 52 executive positions last year, by myself." THAT is superb!! And your listener will definitely remember this.

Researching a Company Prior to a Networking Meeting

Your networking meeting with anybody will be far more effective if you have thoroughly researched their company and show an awareness of trends, regarding their profit and turnover, or acquisitions if any, some of their latest main product launches, their new business initiatives, or you read about their competitive threats. Find out about industry trends as ell, which means that you ought to read the leading national business newspapers on regular basis, so that you are up to date with the latest developments.

You will find it useful, to have read their annual report and could have access to that information on the Stock Exchange if they are a publicly listed company, or alternatively, you will find some financial information in most public libraries, or on the companies websites.

You can also find a lot of organisational information at your local Chamber of Commerce and the various industry associations together with additional industry specific information.

The Stock Exchange libraries are well worth visiting for comprehensive details on companies listed on the Exchange and for specific reports for which a small fee is payable. It is also possible to key into their computers.

The Networking Meeting: Some Basic Points

Your main objective in the networking meeting must be very clear in your mind from the outset, and must be made equally clear to your contact. You are there to obtain information and advice, not a job. Networking is a marketing activity. Interviewing is a selling activity. If it becomes appropriate to switch from the former to the latter, it must be handled properly, or you will appear to be operating under false pretences.

There are few hard and fast rules on how to conduct a networking meeting. However, following is a suggested format for a typical meeting:

Connect. Take a couple of minutes to establish rapport. You may start with some small talk by commenting on when you last met. Obviously, it's wise to avoid going into how and why you were retrenched or resigned – that's all in the past

1. **Suggest an agenda.** Propose an agenda and at the same time check as to how busy your contact is. Suggest a time limit – you promised to be brief. Make it clear you're not there to ask them for or to see if they know where you can find a job. Instead,

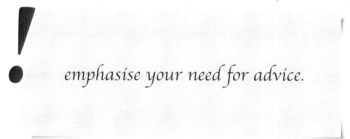

emphasise your need for advice.

   Focus on this and don't worry about "missing out" on a job that may exist. If the person knows of a job for which you may be appropriately qualified, it will surface when the time is right. It's important to strike a confident and eager note (sit on the edge of your chair to give that appearance). Make some observations about your contact's company and mention that you are seeking their advice because they are particularly knowledgeable as regards that industry.

2. **Bring up your objective.** Outline your job objective and your marketing strategy. Mention the types of jobs or industries and companies in which you are interested. For example, you may need to say something like

> *"My objective is to become a Sales Director. Most recently, my positions have been.... Some of my achievements have been... I see little opportunity for growth at... (your present employer), and I've decided to assess other opportunities that might be more appropriate to my goals."*

3. **Request to have your resume reviewed.** The previous step will elicit a response which will enable you to give your resume, in order to assess your potential "fit" for the industries or companies you've mentioned. Ask the executive to review your resume. Expand on a few of your skills and achievements and convey what you believe you can contribute to a new employer. Remember, you want to become part of their network. You want them to be an extra set of eyes and ears in your job search. However, remember also that you are "information gathering" and should not sell. Offer to leave a copy of your resume with your contact. After he or she has reviewed it, ask

> *"Now that you have a better idea about my background, do you see a good fit for the area I want to be in?"*

If the response is affirmative, ask for any suggestions they may have as to how these can be maximised, or in the alternative response, how the obstacles can be minimised or eliminated.

4. **Get Referrals.** Aim to obtain at least two referrals. If your contact has a challenge in suggesting names, do mention or repeat a few of the companies in which you are interested or a few with which your contact's company is likely to have business with and this will help them remember some names. You could also make a request like:

> *"I am seeking to meet people who can help me continue the process of building a contact network and who can add to the information I already have gathered. Networking is such an important part of my campaign, who do you know what would be the kind of person I should contact?"*

Your network will definitely continue to expand if you deliberately set out at every meeting to obtain <u>an average of two further contacts.</u> Your networking activity can wither or halt only if you lose interest. If you're between jobs, remember career search should be a forty hour a week activity.

5. **Increase your companies/target list.** Ask

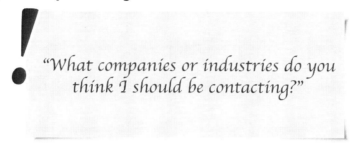

"What companies or industries do you think I should be contacting?"

If no suggestions are offered, show your contact or target list. Ask if they know any of the companies or people listed. This step can be an excellent means of jolting anyone's memory and gaining contacts in other organisations that you have targeted, or referrals to people you have identified.

6. **Be grateful.** Thank them for their time, interest and suggestions. Conclude by suggesting that, in appreciation of their help, you'll telephone them in several weeks to let them know how things are going in your search.
After the meeting, you should make a written record of all the details for subsequent follow up. And you should immediately send a letter/email of thanks, as previously mentioned.

Never pass up an opportunity to network. It's a compliment to ask another person for assistance. Talk to as many people as you can. Don't underestimate their value to you.

Set weekly goals for yourself, and then make sure you get out and carry them through! Your results will be good as you make them.

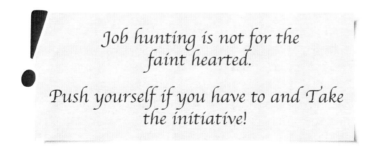

Job hunting is not for the faint hearted.

Push yourself if you have to and Take the initiative!

Here are a few points to remember:

>**Do** leave a copy of your resume at each networking meeting.

>**Do** ask your contact in the meeting if you may use their name when approaching the contacts they have suggested.

>**Do** write, immediately after the meeting, thanking them for their time and help. This should be done the same day whilst you are fresh in their mind. They have done you a considerable favour, after all. As with all correspondence in career search, mark it

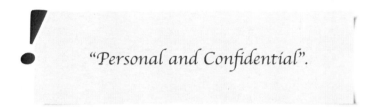

"Personal and Confidential".

It will then be opened by its intended recipient, not the secretary.

Here is a sample letter of thanks after a networking meeting:

Strictly Private and Confidential

Dear Simon,

Thank you again for meeting with me today. Your input and suggestions on my career objectives and my resume were of great value to me.

The information you gave me regarding .... was most helpful. I appreciate your recommendation that I contact Mark Smith for further suggestions. I will also be following up with the other individuals you suggested and will be making contact with the companies you mentioned.

Thanks again. I now know why Jake Blog holds you in such high esteem. Please keep my objectives in mind in case you hear of other opportunities. As we discussed, I will be back in touch with you in a few weeks to see if you have any further suggestions and to keep you informed of my progress.

Sincerely,

....

Remember to keep records of your networking meetings. There is no harm in ringing your contacts again in a couple of months to let them know how your situation has developed, and they'll be interested to know how you go on with the leads they suggested. Be aware there is a fine line between too much follow-up and not enough. Only you can judge this and it will vary depending on the "chemistry" of each meeting.

Target Companies and Individuals

The more you network, the more you will notice that the same names of companies are been suggested by your contacts. You would have researched these as well as similar / competition/aligned/ complementary companies. You will find that a list of companies is emerging, where perceive you could make a contribution and where, you would like to work. The justifications would have developed as you worked on your list.

Your next step will be to identify in each company the executive who has the capacity to hire you. This will always be the line manager immediately above the position you are seeking. This information is readily available on the company's website, or alternatively, do call the receptionist, befriend her and ask her who that executive is.

What you need to do next, is to making a point of checking with the people with whom you are having networking meetings whether they know "..Name of Person........" (Name the person in one of your preferred companies with the capability of hiring you).

In your earliest networking meetings you were eager to hear of any possible contacts from which you could develop networking lines.

However, with your previous meetings and your own research, your thoughts have crystallised so in your networking meetings you should start to be more proactive by **deliberately raising the names of these companies and asking your contacts if they know your target executive.**

You will be surprised how quickly you find a networking contact who knows the key person who could hire you in one of your targeted companies. This is the break you need. You should telephone them along very similar lines to previous networking calls:

> *"Good morning, Mr. Smith! I'm Peter Hunt , a friend of Marie Stafford, who says she knows you well and mentioned that she felt sure you would be able to help me. Do you have a minute? (Wait for an affirmative response).*
>
> *Great! I am currently exploring new career opportunities. For the last four years I've been General Manager at .... Prior to that, I spent five years as a National Sales Manager. I would really appreciate it if I could see you for twenty minutes. I am sure that with your experience in the .... industry you would be able to help me with your views on the industry's progress, its trends, and the opportunities in the next eighteen months and over the long term. **I am developing a few strategies and would like to get your advice and comments.** I would also appreciate it if you could look through my resume and **I feel sure you would be able to suggest a couple of people to contact** and a few companies to think about. I would be happy to see you outside normal working hours if that would help. How about six o'clock one evening?"*

Note the same phrases recurring. The **compliment and the unambiguous request for help**! You are suggesting that the contact should read your resume, and that you have confidence in their ability to come up with meaningful suggestions. With this approach, there is no likelihood of making them feel defensive or that you are putting them on the spot because what you really want is a job in their company.

This is how you can successfully networker, by following this scenario and talking warmly and confidently on the phone. This would achieve a 90% success rate in securing meetings despite the pressures that your target has in their jobs.

> *People are usually happy to help, provide advice, keep an eye open for you and share a few names.*

Obviously, you will come across individuals on your target list that nobody you contact seems to personally. In such case, do some research about who you think is likely to have a business or social relationship with that person.

Consider that the person might be well known to one of their supplier companies. Find someone on your contact list who is likely to know the Supply Director or the Purchasing Manager of that company. Phone your contact and then phone the person he or she suggests and establish a networking meeting.

Target Networking Meeting

The procedures for the target networking meeting is basically as previously explained. Before you meet your target networking contact, however, it is essential that you research their company very thoroughly. You want to show a keen understanding of the company and its affairs, leaving them to deduce that you can make a contribution.

Networking Email/Letter Font

When other means of accessing the hidden market are not available and if your situation requires sending a letter or an email, there are specific techniques that can be utilised with a well constructed introductory letter.

You will need for this letter to be well constructed, following the principles of networking, where personalisation is most important. This means creating and building on personal relationships to ensure that your approach is not "cold".

Introduction

In your introduction, you MUST gain immediate attention.

Here are a couple of examples you could use:

I spoke Peter Larkin, yesterday, who suggested that I contact you

Or

Yesterday, I met with Peter Larkin, who suggested that I contact you

Or

Our mutual acquaintance, Janette Goodyear, suggested that I contact you

Or

I recently came across an article in which you were quoted, that was of great interest to me

Body

In the body of your letter, you must mention at least one interesting idea, which is new and related to your type of work. That will identify you as a stimulating person to meet, and make the recipient want to become acquainted with you.

Or

You could list several achievements relating to the type of position you are seeking, ensuring that you are quantifying your statements in this regard.

Conclusion

Be positive, tell the recipient that you will call to set up a meeting for a mutually convenient time, in a couple of days' time. Keep the time of your call close to when you sent the letter, so that it remains fresh in the recipient's mind.

Keep you letter to one page maximum.

Here is a sample to copy:

Date

Strictly Private and Confidential

Dear John,

You knowledge of the ……………….industry and of business in the "Town" area is renown.

I believe that you might be able to help me with answers to some questions I have about the ………..
area. I am writing to you as I trust that you may be willing to grant me a few minutes in this regard.

Since 1998, I have worked as a General manager with XUZ Company and my responsibilities have
involved P&L for the company, managing a team of 45 direct reports and a budget of $127Mios.

Use Bullet points to highlights some areas that are likely to be of interest

I will be in …..….. *town* ……... for the week commencing …..….. and would very much appreciate
the opportunity to meeting with you to get some advice and direction as to what activity in ……...
town ……... is relevant to my background.

I would also welcome the opportunity to share ideas of mutual professional interest.

I will call you in a couple of days to arrange a mutually convenient time so that we can exchange
some information.

I look forward to meeting with you

Yours Sincerely,

…………….

From Networking Meeting to Interview

You might find that at some point during the meeting, your contact's body language and the flavour of the conversation may change. Your contact may start to ask interview style questions, and to relate aspects of your achievements and skills to some unknown requirements.

In this case one of two things is happening. Either your contact doesn't understand that you are sincerely there to benefit from their advice and enlist their support and not to seek employment in their organisation, or he or she does understand your intentions but wants to interview you anyway.

If you think they misunderstood your intention, then you must immediately clarify the situation, so that they understand that you have genuinely come for information and help and that you did not expect an interview. This will get the situation out into the open so you both know where you stand.

However, if they genuinely have a job in mind then it is best for both of you to know that and proceed in normal interview fashion. This will be your chance to respond as you would in an interview. Tell them how you have researched their company and its industry, prospects and short and long term opportunities and then outline your achievements, skills and the contribution you believe you can make.

For a networking meeting to turn into a successful interview:

1.   You must NOT initiate the change.
2.   You must DETERMINE if the change is the result of a misunderstanding and make a good faith effort to keep it a networking meeting.
3.   You must LABEL THE CHANGE once it seems imminent or desirable.

Remember that networking allows a person to be evaluated by the contact even when no job exists. Sometimes an individual can create a job for themselves. Let your expectations, talents, personality and attitude shine through. Because you are so well focused, they may want you for their team.

How Is Networking in Today's Economic Environment

There has been no better time for networking than the present. Most companies downsized substantially and there are numerous companies who admit they overdid their downsizing. Now, there are many Chief Executive Officers, Presidents, Managing Directors, General Managers and Divisional Managers with half-formulated plans in their mind for projects to be developed. Some will have completed plans just waiting for implementation when the environment improves sufficiently.

When you entertain a networking meeting it could well be that you strike a chord with your contact. Your set of skills and achievements reminds them of a project they have longed for somebody to complete. But their lean management team was so stretched that they felt they could not in all fairness delegate and expect that size of project to be given adequate priority. Now you have appeared on the scene. They offer you a three-month contract to undertake this project – perhaps with the option of permanent employment under certain conditions. You will be eager to take it since project work offers so many advantages: less concern about your diminishing savings, greater self esteem, an improved platform for interviews, more opportunities for networking, the possibility of permanent employment with the same company. Alternatively, your contact could arrange a second meeting and then offer permanent employment.

Is this possible? YES!

Personal Story

My own work history, which prompted the writing of this book, ran along those lines. When my position was made redundant in July 2009, I was unable to secure a permanent role, as the economy had just its greatest negative impact at that time. I started wondering if I should look into the contractual market as well, something I had never done before. Very soon thereafter, I was offered a 2 months contract, with possible extension. I ended up staying in that company for over a year, when I was approached by another organisation about a permanent position.

Remember that around 80% of executive positions and management jobs are never advertised.

Remember also that competition for these positions is far less than for those advertised in the press. Sometimes you may be one of only a few who know about the vacancy. On occasions you may be the only one.

In my situation, I was interviewed by two people, subsequently received a call from the chairman two hours later and he hired me on the phone, to start working the following Monday, which is when I first met him face to face!

> *It is common for networkers to find jobs are actually triggered and created by their meeting. This is particularly so for contract work.*

In reality, networking is easy since it is evolutionary. You start with your friends, relatives and close acquaintances and develop your telephone style and your meeting tactics with them. Next, you do the same with your less well-known contacts. Then comes the first time you need to call somebody you've been recommended to contact but have never met before. Use a few prompt notes and make sure that you mention the mutual contact at the start of the conversation. The best thing is to line up several of these and call them one after the other. This will help you to gather momentum and develop a flair with your calls. Use the same technique when telephoning one of your targets.

A high percentage of people will see you, for one or more of the following reasons: they are flattered that you are seeking their advice; it can expand **their** network; the meeting may provide them with fresh ideas; and you may have mentioned a mutual friend to whom they feel obligated.

A by-product of networking is that you will develop a confidence in using the telephone that will always stay with you.

> *Remember the key rules of networking.*
> *Never ask for a job; always ask for suggestions.*
> *Don't ask for favours; always ask for advice.*
>
> *Finally, you must remember that career searching is a numbers game.*

If you are between jobs in particular, you can make this fact work for you by using your time to make new contacts in the manner outlined above. Set yourself a realistic goal, such as fifteen contact visits per week, and stick to it. Look at this activity as a new phase of your career. It can be a highly productive and satisfying one!

Putting in the Effort

ARE YOU REALLY putting in the effort it takes to succeed?

Reported in Weddles's excellent newsletter are the following statistics from a 2010 survey reported in The Economist:

Length of time Unemployed Workers Spend Looking for a Job (per day)

- U.K.: 10 minutes
- Sweden: 10 minutes
- Germany: 10 minutes
- Spain: 20-30 minutes
- France: 20-30 minutes
- U.S.: 40 minutes
- Australia : 40 minutes

In 10-40 minutes per day, what can you accomplish? Surf the web for the latest postings... dash off a couple of resumes... call one contact and give up when he or she has no leads for you. But just think what you could do if you devoted 2, 4, 6, or even 8 hours of your day to your job search - strategies and activities that will expand your horizons, your opportunities, and your results.

- Prepare and practice your "elevator pitch" so you can smoothly and confidently deliver it during an interview, at a formal networking event, or to a casually met acquaintance.
- Write out your greatest career "success stories" and practice relating them in a clear, compelling manner.

- Create a list of 50 people you can contact and make 10 phone calls per day to complete the list in a week. (Use your new elevator pitch for best results.) Make a new list next week.
- Review your resume and cover letters and edit/polish to perfection.
- Identify and research 10 companies that might be a good fit for you. Use LinkedIn and/or your personal network to connect to decision makers (or anyone) at those companies.
- Pick up the phone and call them! Use your referral as an introduction, then deliver a brief message about your potential value to the company. Ask for a meeting.
- Start a new list of companies next week.
- Read a book or online articles about trends in interviewing. Think about how you'll respond, and practice your answers to tough questions.
- Review your interview wardrobe and replace, repair, polish, mend, or iron anything that looks less than perfect.
- Identify your top value points that you'll want to communicate in your next interview. Focus on value to the company, not interest to you.
- Make an interview "cheat sheet" of your top value points and keywords for your success stories. Practice your interview responses using just the crib sheet.
- Call someone you know who's unemployed and ask if you can be of help.

I could go on, but by now, I am sure that you get the point.

> **!** *Work the process and you'll reap the rewards.*

Resume Templates

Business Development – Marketing – Operations

EXECUTIVE PROFILE

- **Relationship Management**
- **Business Process Outsourcing**
- **Business Development**
- **Revenue & Profit Enhancement**

Strategic and growth-oriented leader with broad expertise in business development, marketing, operations, and consultative solution-selling; 15-year track record of identifying and capturing new business opportunities, developing and maintaining marquee client relationships, and aligning products/ services with strategic markets.

Sharp business focus complemented by customer orientation and strong foundation in strategic business - technology solutions. Deep expertise in outsourcing and offshore IT solutions for multiple industries.

Highest levels of integrity, ethics, business judgment, work ethic, and maturity.

- Strategic Planning / Tactical Execution / P&L
- Business Plans / M&A / Venture Capital
- Strategic Alliance & Channel Development
- Business & Technology Liaison
- Rainmaker Marketing Expertise
- Customer Acquisition, Retention & Extension
- Customer, Vendor & Partner Relationship Management
- Deal Structuring & Contract Negotiation
- Cross-Functional Team Leadership
- Quantitative & Business Analysis

EXECUTIVE TEAM COMMENTARY

…Broad business perspective and extremely strong business acumen… The ability to architect and drive change… Action orientation with strong execution skills and drive for results… Strong influencing skills and tremendous personal energy and edge… Passion of a successful entrepreneur and the discipline of a seasoned executive… Externally competitive and internally team-oriented.

PROFESSIONAL EXPERIENCE

■ **VP BUSINESS DEVELOPMENT**   **International IT Services,** USA 2003–Present

Created and executed successful refocus/repositioning strategy for business services outsourcing firm.

- Drove revenues up 100% first year, 150% in last 18 months. Increased operating margins 25%.
- Increased operating efficiency 40% and improved client satisfaction scores from 75% to 98%.
- Generated $12MM VC funding. Participated in M&A analysis, selection, and integration (company purchased in fourth quarter 2005).

■ **BUSINESS DEVELOPMENT DIRECTOR**   **Giantdata Systems USA** 2002–2003

In interim executive role, ignited stalled business through fresh ideas and innovative approaches to business turnaround, marketing, branding, product positioning, and pricing. Grew product revenue to 35% of total sales.

■ **FOUNDER / CEO**   **Overseas Solutions,** India, 1999–2002

- Built successful offshore IT services firm, connecting US firms with Southeast Asian providers.
- Achieved exceptional customer satisfaction, earning repeat business from 90% of clients.
- Negotiated sale of the firm at 600% return on initial investment.

■ **ASSISTANT /ASSOCIATE BRAND MANAGER**   **Procter & Gamble** USA, India, 1990–1999
GLOBAL PROJECT LEADER

EDUCATION

MBA, 1995: UBM University—New York

BS, Computer Science, 1992: UBM University—New Yok

BS, Business Administration, 1990: Cornell University—New Jersey

VP SALES • REGIONAL / NATIONAL SALES MANAGER

Excel in building high-performing sales organizations and transforming stagnant sales to vibrant growth.

Unbroken record of top performance in sales, sales management, and development of national sales force to achieve aggressive goals. Demonstrated proficiency in all areas of executive sales leadership—vision through strategies, tactical plans, compensation programs, communication protocols, and reporting structures. Proven ability to lead start-up, restructured, and existing sales organizations and to create customer-focused, solution-selling culture.

Areas of proven performance:

- Driving long-term vision while attaining short-term financial results
- Turning around underperforming teams and organizations; achieving rapid and sustainable growth
- Developing sales skills/improving sales performance through training, mentoring, and one-on-one coaching
- Creating highly efficient and productive operations

PROFESSIONAL EXPERIENCE & ACHIEVEMENTS

■ **GENERAL REVENUE CORPORATION,** Division of Sallie Mae New York • 2002–2006

Collections service organization specializing in home mortgage defaults; #1 industry leader with a substantial client portfolio of banks, credit unions, and mortgage lenders in 50 states. Acquired by Citigroup from original founders/private owners in 2003.

VP SALES & MARKETING

Recruited to take sales to a new level, transformed unfocused organization with stalled revenues to a dynamic team that virtually doubled business in 4 years. Invigorated sales team by defining vision and introducing the strategies, programs, and tools to achieve it. Fully accountable for revenue performance and management of sales, marketing, and client service. Led a team of 16 direct/indirect reports.

- Delivered dramatic growth, hitting new company records for sales volume every year.

	Placement Volume	Revenue	# of Clients
2005	$460M	$36M	985
2003	$341M	$30M	715
2001	$206M	$24M	490

- Achieved stellar results via a lean organization, increasing productivity of sales force 33% during tenure.
- Clearly established brand image and value to drive continuous growth and exceptional client retention.
- Developed trade show strategy and exhibits focusing on returns to customers (e.g., in 2004, returned more than $100M to clients); oversaw participation in 60+ trade shows annually.

- Improved communication with the sales force; boosted morale and results through carefully structured compensation plans that rewarded the achievement of strategic business goals.
- Retained to lead sales following acquisition, transitioned rapidly and successfully to new ownership and took on new responsibility for marketing, contract bidding, and client service.

■ **REAL SOLUTIONS,** Division of Intercontinental Corp.   North America • 1988–2002

Industry's leading provider of commercial real estate information—paper/electronic sales leads and analytics, serving more than a million customers in the $3.4 trillion global real estate community.

SENIOR SALES DIRECTOR / NORTH AMERICA, NATIONAL ACCOUNTS, 1/01–5/02

Grew revenues 20% annually, staving off competition through focus on value and service to top-tier national accounts in the U.S. and Canada. Led 75-member international sales organization, creating the sales strategies to achieve aggressive corporate goals and managing plans, programs, contracts, expenses, reporting, trade-show activity, and team performance.

- Retained #1 market position and delivered 20% growth in an increasingly competitive/price-sensitive market.
- Introduced "gold" customer concept that rewarded best accounts while boosting sales penetration.
- Devised new reporting protocols that streamlined reporting processes and delivered more usable information.
- Guided sales managers in setting "stretch" yet achievable goals for sales team.
- Boosted morale of sales managers and field sales force through positive teambuilding and one-on-one coaching.

SENIOR SALES DIRECTOR / EASTERN U.S., 4/00–12/01

Successfully transitioned "turf" coverage to team coverage, leading streamlined/restructured sales organization to healthy revenue growth. Promoted to lead newly combined Regional and National Accounts sales teams, 7 sales managers and 78 reps covering the eastern half of the United States. Fully accountable for revenue performance and all sales/management functions, from planning, goal setting, and reporting through team member training and motivation.

- Achieved 10% year-over-year sales growth.
- Created joint regional/national selling initiatives while introducing internal telesales for the first time in company history. Retained nearly 100% of staff during challenging transition and created true team chemistry.
- Introduced new reporting and communication protocols that emphasized joint sales calls and internal partnerships to drive solution selling strategies.

SALES MANAGER, NATIONAL ACCOUNTS, 12/99–4/00

Exceeded 100% of aggressive sales goals, leading 12-member National Accounts team in selling to and servicing large corporate customers in 8-state Northeast region. Managed sales reporting, staff assignments, and expense budgets. Set sales goals, created motivational sales contests, and worked with sales reps to improve selling skills.

- Engaged each member of 12-person sales team, defining individual goals and creating success plans that resulted in top team and individual performance—including #1 U.S. Sales Rep in 1998.
- Negotiated and/or approved all major sales contracts.

SALES TRAINING SPECIALIST, EASTERN U.S., 1/97–12/99

Hand-picked to build and lead an elite training organization to introduce a radically different technology-based product line to the regional sales force. Recommended selection of 3 team members; built team concept; defined goals and compensation plan; created team structure and communications protocol. Traveled extensively, working side-by-side with sales reps and coaching/empowering them in new sales strategies for innovative product.

- Achieved unqualified success: New product delivered $10M revenue in 2 years, 2X initial goal.
- All team members were subsequently promoted to Sales Management roles.

NATIONAL ACCOUNTS REPRESENTATIVE, Boston, MA • 1993–1997

REGIONAL SALES REPRESENTATIVE, Buffalo, NY • 1989–1993

SALES SERVICE REPRESENTATIVE, Providence, RI • 1988–1989

EDUCATION

UNIVERSITY OF RHODE ISLAND, Kingston, RI

- BS Business Administration, 1992

COMMUNITY LEADERSHIP

- Advisory Board Member, The Country Club, Brookline, MA, 2000–Present
- Youth sports coach (baseball and basketball), Waltham Recreation Leagues, 1989–2000

JOHN CITIZEN **Business Development** CONTACT DETAILS

EXECUTIVE PROFILE

- **Relationship Management**
- **Business Process Outsourcing**
- **Business Development**
- **Revenue & Profit Enhancement**

Strategic and growth-oriented leader with broad expertise in business development, marketing, operations, and consultative solution-selling; 15-year track record of identifying and capturing new business opportunities, developing and maintaining marquee client relationships, and aligning products/ services with strategic markets.

Sharp business focus complemented by customer orientation and strong foundation in strategic business technology solutions. Deep expertise in outsourcing and offshore IT solutions for multiple industries. Highest levels of integrity, ethics, business judgment, work ethic, and maturity.

- Strategic Planning / Tactical Execution / P&L
- Business Plans / M&A / Venture Capital
- Strategic Alliance & Channel DevelopmentManagement
- Business & Technology Liaison
- Rainmaker Marketing Expertise
- Quantitative & Business Analysis
- Customer Acquisition, Retention & Extension
- Customer, Vendor & Partner Relationship
- Deal Structuring & Contract Negotiation
- Cross-Functional Team Leadership

EXECUTIVE TEAM COMMENTARY EXECUTIVE TEAM COMMENTARY

…Broad business perspective and extremely strong business acumen… The ability to architect and drive change… Action orientation with strong execution skills and drive for results… Strong influencing skills and tremendous personal energy and edge… Passion of a successful entrepreneur and the discipline of a seasoned executive… Externally competitive and internally team-oriented.

PROFESSIONAL EXPERIENCE

- **VP BUSINESS DEVELOPMENT – Brilliant IT Services Company 2003 – Present**

    - Created and executed successful refocus/repositioning strategy for business services outsourcing firm.
    - Drove revenues up 100% first year, 150% in last 18 months. Increased operating margins 25%.
    - Increased operating efficiency 40% and improved client satisfaction scores from 75% to 98%.
    - Generated $12MM VC funding. Participated in M&A analysis, selection, and integration (company purchased in fourth quarter 2005).

- **BUSINESS DEVELOPMENT DIRECTOR Microinfo IT Systems 2002 – 2003**

  In interim executive role, ignited stalled business through fresh ideas and innovative approaches to business turnaround, marketing, branding, product positioning, and pricing. Grew product revenue to 35% of total sales.

- **FOUNDER / CEO Foreign IT Solutions, company USA and India 1999–2002**
  - Built successful offshore IT services firm, connecting US firms with Southeast Asian providers.
  - Achieved exceptional customer satisfaction, earning repeat business from 90% of clients.
  - Negotiated sale of the firm at 600% return on initial investment.

- **BRAND MANAGER Proctor & Gamble 1991 - 1998**
  - Global Project Leader – USA and India

EDUCATION

MBA – Cincinati University 1989

BS, Computer Science Cincinatti University 1990

BS, Business Administration Oxford University 1993

CHIEF EXECUTIVE OFFICER

Multinational Fortune 500 Companies · Public & Private Global Enterprises
Accomplished executive with a flawless record of improving profits, building brands, and creating shareholder value:

- **Biva:** Transformation to #1 market share, highest profitability and equity valuation in its marketplace, and largest US-owned brand portfolio.
- **Lands, Inc.:** Reversal of 4-year slide to 114% increase in stock value.
- **Trye Company:** Best sales and profit in company history.
- **Maxi Foods:** First sales growth and earnings increase in 3 years.
- **DynaFoods:** Increase in sales and profits 3X, stock price from $8 to $85.
- **Value Creation**
- **Brand & Portfolio Building**
- **High-Growth Phase Management**
- **Turnarounds: Financial & Operational Restructuring**
- **Mergers & Acquisitions**

EXPERIENCE AND ACCOMPLISHMENTS

Biva International   California, 1999–Present
$300M multi-brand, multi-channel, global optical and jewelry company
CHAIRMAN, PRESIDENT, AND CEO

Built the largest, most profitable company in its marketplace. Transformed unprofitable, illiquid, debt-defaulted company into a thriving corporation with world-recognized brands and the highest equity valuation of all companies in its sector. Developed an exceptional management team and a company-wide culture of performance excellence.

Brand Building
- Created the largest US-owned optical brand portfolio by focusing growth strategy on high-value brands, divesting non-core businesses, and driving strategic acquisitions.
- Developed ByView to the top-selling sunglass brand, recognized among Top 100 Best Known Brands and Top 10 Accessories Brands by *Women's Wear Daily*.
- Achieved #1 market position for multiple product lines:
  - Sunglasses—improved from #3 to #1 with a 32% share.
  - Reading glasses—dominated the market with 47% share, #1 and #2 brands (ByVision and CoolVu).
- Licensed Levi's, Body Glove, Champion, other high-value brands to position Byva for sustainable growth.
- Revitalized the "Byva Viewers" advertising campaign, ranked in Top 100 Advertising Campaigns by *Advertising Age*. Brought on new celebrity endorsers Shania Twain and Nick Lachey.

Strategic Growth

- Successfully entered new markets (prescription frames, premium sunglasses) and built to 5% of sales by year 2.
- Turned around international division from earnings loss to the most profitable business in the company.
- Increased sales 15% and profits 33% annually and earned the leading market share in key countries.
- Transformed jewelry business from revenue and profit declines to double-digit revenue growth and profitability.
- Successfully acquired and integrated 2 companies, including 4 brands, in one year.

Financial and Operational Improvements

- Built the strongest capital structure in the industry. Completed all acquisitions without equity infusion.
- Built award-winning supply chain system, achieving 98% order accuracy and 99% on-time performance.

Lands, Inc.   Chicago, IL, 1996–1999
$600M Fortune 500 multi-brand company (NYSE)
EXECUTIVE VICE PRESIDENT

Brought on board to drive across-the-board performance improvements following 16 straight quarters of declining sales and profits. Provided vision and leadership to develop and execute successful turnaround and growth strategy.

Growth & Profit Performance

- Doubled stock value from $7 to $15 per share.
- Increased sales and profits each quarter in 4 straight years.

Strategic Brand Building

- Defined core expertise as footwear brand management and increased brand portfolio from 3 to 7 brands; added powerful marketing value by licensing such brands as Tommy Hilfiger and Levi's.
- Restored vibrancy and vitality to 3 legacy brands. Improved products, revamped advertising, raised prices, and drove up profits.

Trye Company   Los Angeles, CA, 1995–1996
$125M footwear and apparel manufacturer (OTC)
CHIEF OPERATING OFFICER (1995–1996)
MEMBER, BOARD OF DIRECTORS (1994–1996)

Recruited from Board for interim leadership role, achieved highest sales and profit in company history. Streamlined operations, improved profitability, and implemented operational systems and computer-based supply/demand matching that delivered the right products to the right places on time.

- Cut product costs 40% by increasing overseas production.
- Predicted and counteracted retail downturn—prevented losses by canceling 20% of factory orders, reducing expenses 12%, and eliminating $3M in excess inventory.

Maxi Foods   Los Angeles, CA, 1994–1995
$2B multinational consumer products and retail company (NYSE)
CHIEF FINANCIAL OFFICER AND EXECUTIVE VICE PRESIDENT

Accepted 1-year restructuring challenge from a Wall Street pioneer and exceeded all expectations in positioning company for successful sale. Achieved first earnings increase in 3 years. Resolved liquidity crisis by jump-starting sales, eliminating shipping backlog, and reducing expenses.

Dynafoods, Inc.   Atlanta, GA, 1990–1994
$500M footwear and apparel wholesale and retail company
SENIOR VICE PRESIDENT

Planned and executed brand and operating strategy that resulted in Dynagoods' highest growth years. Repositioned brand to premium channels and price points. Built company-owned retail store chain. Initiated apparel business and positioned the brand overseas.

- Increased stock price from $8 to $85 by growing sales and profits 3X.
- Fourth best-performing stock on NYSE; recognized as most successful financial turnaround by Wall Street.
- Improved ROE from 9.8% to 21.5%.

Experience Prior to 1990

- Southern Department Stores, Inc.: Vice President and Treasurer
- Adair, Inc.: Chief Financial Officer / General Manager, Altamare Division
- Sanfils, Inc.: Vice President and Treasurer / President, San Enterprises, Inc. (division)
- GM Finance Corporation: General Manager
- General Motors: Financial Analyst

EDUCATION AND HONORS

MBA, Graduate School of Business, Stanford University, Stanford, CA

BA Economics, Emory University, Atlanta, GA

PROFESSIONAL DISTINCTIONS

Board of Directors, Adair, Inc.

Author, *Financial Strategies for Privately Held Companies* (Jossey-Bass, 1995)

MILITARY SERVICE

Army Officer

CEO — CFO — GENERAL MANAGER

Strategic and hands-on executive, highly skilled in creating and executing blueprints for business growth. Consistent career record of achieving profitability, cost control, and operational improvement in highly challenging environments. Talent for building teams and instilling customer focus. Extensive international experience (multilingual, multicultural). Proactive and nimble in fast-paced, rapidly changing environments.

- Strategic Planning & Tactical Execution
- Financial Planning & Analysis
- P&L Management
- Cost Control & Profit Enhancement
- Multi-Site Operations Management
- Accounting & MIS System Implementation
- Staff Training, Development & Advancement
- Customer Relationship Management

EXPERIENCE AND ACHIEVEMENTS

International FOOD, Cleves, OH ($40MM food-service provider to offshore and land-based facilities) 2004–2007

- **President and CEO**

Revitalized the company. Stepping into interim "rescue" assignment, preserved key contracts, improved financial and operational performance, increased customer satisfaction, and created strategic and tactical blueprints for continued success and growth of the company.

- Retained 2 major accounts—23% of total sales volume—by boosting visibility, customer contact, and customer service.
- Swiftly reduced food costs 2% and administrative labor expenses 3.5% by introducing accurate expense-monitoring systems.
- Increased client satisfaction level from 60% to 93%.
- Turned around lackluster financial organization, reengineered the internal-controls structure, and created a smooth-functioning unit supporting 23 clients in 119 locations.
- Enhanced training, communication, staff selection and performance.

WORLDWIDE SERVICES, Florence, KY ($500MM provider of support services to remote sites)   1994–2004

- **VP, South & Central America,   99–04 / International Operations Manager,   97–99**

Opened international markets for the company, repeatedly taking on new challenges for organization in transition. Delivered consistently superior profitability in intensely competitive markets and volatile global sites.

Concurrently managed as many as 16 branches providing food service to mining camps, oil refineries, construction operations, oil rigs/platforms, military camps, and administrative offices in countries throughout Central and South America, Caribbean, Europe, and Africa. Developed strategic and tactical plans for marketing and mobilization of each new branch; managed P&L and financial performance; maintained client relationships through hands-on supervision at worldwide jobsites.

- Developed high-volume, high-profit business in South America: Venezuela from start-up to $60MM revenue, 60% market share; Brazil to $18MM revenue, 35% market share.
- Identified lucrative market segment and led business expansion serving US military operations in Bosnia and Haiti.

- **Corporate Controller, 94–97**

Supervised worldwide financial and accounting functions for more than 85 national and international branches. Directly managed the company's operations in Nigeria.

- Reorganized finance and data-processing departments to improve efficiency, timeliness, and relevance of financial reporting; reduced staffing cost by $24K.
- Standardized financial and jobsite reporting worldwide.
- Transformed warehouse into an operational distribution profit center.

TECH STOP, INC., Indianapolis, IN ($80MM multi-site electronics retailer)   1991–1994

- **Chief Financial Officer and VP of Finance**

Directed 38-member team in financial, administrative, and sales-forecasting functions for all 20 stores in the company. Reported to President and Board of Directors.

- Saved more than $200K in sales-tax audit by accurately reconstructing 3 years of sales and franchise taxes.
- Erased an 18-month financial-reporting backlog in 4 months.
- Automated accounting functions, enabling 23% productivity increase and 30% reduction in labor.
- Saved $18K annually in audit fees.
- Captured $3MM previously lost revenue through aggressive attention to manufacturer rebate programs.

EARLY CAREER

- **President, BeckLaay Accounting Services,** Indianapolis, IN, 87–91
  - Launched and managed accounting practice serving medium and small businesses. Grew business to 63 clients and negotiated its profitable sale.
- **Assistant Controller/Credit Manager,** Acte Supplies, Indianapolis, IN, 84–87
  - Improved performance of the financial organization—reduced reporting times, shrank A/R and delinquent accounts, and cut costs. Drove conversion from manual to computerized accounting, invoicing, and inventory-control systems.
- **Senior Audit Manager,** AturnoPerez Associates, CPA Firm, Belize, 80–83
  - Managed audits for manufacturing and industrial clients of this Central American representative for Touche Ross & Thouborn.

PROFESSIONAL PROFILE

EDUCATION   BSBA (concentration in Accounting), 1984—Indiana University

TECHNOLOGY

Real World Accounting	IBM System 34
Peachtree Complete Accounting	AS/400
Lotus 1-2-3	Hyperion
MS Office	JD Edwards

ADDITIONAL   Global citizen and road warrior—regularly spending more than 50% of time traveling to and residing in South America, Caribbean, Central America, and Europe. Fluent Spanish and Brazilian Portuguese; conversational Yugoslavian/Croatian Bosnian.

GLOBAL SERVICES,

- ### Corporate Controller 1994–1997

  Supervised worldwide financial and accounting functions for more than 72 national and international branches. Directly managed the company's operations in Algeria.

  - Reorganized finance and data-processing departments to improve efficiency, timeliness, and relevance of financial reporting; reduced staffing cost by $37K.
  - Standardized financial and jobsite reporting worldwide.
  - Transformed warehouse into an operational distribution profit center.

- ### Zat ELECTRICS 1991–1994
  Sydney, Australia IN ($60M multi-site electronics retailer)

  Chief Financial Officer and VP of Finance

  Directed 28-member team in financial, administrative, and sales-forecasting functions for all 35 stores in the company. Reported to President and Board of Directors.

  - Saved more than $150K in sales-tax audit by accurately reconstructing 4 years of sales and franchise taxes.
  - Eliminated an 18-month financial-reporting backlog in 3 months.
  - Automated accounting functions, enabling 35% productivity increase and 30% reduction in labour.
  - Saved $20K annually in audit fees.
  - Recaptured $4MM revenue through aggressive attention to manufacturer rebate programs.

- ### EARLY CAREER

  Managing Director, CountTrue Accounting Services, Sydney, Australia   1987–1991
  Launched and managed accounting practice serving medium and small businesses.

  Grew business to 120 clients and negotiated its profitable sale.

  Assistant Controller/Credit Manager, Arteme Supplies, Sydney   1984–1987
  Improved performance of the financial organization—reduced reporting times, shrank delinquent accounts, and cut costs. Drove conversion from manual to computerized accounting, invoicing, and inventory-control systems.

  Senior Audit Manager, Olimer and Associates, CPA Firm, Sydney Australia ,   1980–1983
  Managed audits for manufacturing and industrial clients of this representative for Deloitte Touche Tohmatsu

PROFESSIONAL PROFILE

Education: BAcc graduate 1984—U.T.S. University - Sydney

Technology: Real World Accounting   IBM System 34
                   Peachtree Complete Accounting   AS/400
                   Lotus 1-2-3   Hyperion
                   MS Office   JD Edwards

Additional: Global citizen and travel veteran through South and Central America, Europe
                   and Australia
                   Fluent Spanish, Brazilian and French; conversational
                   Dutch/German/Afrikaans/Swahili.

STRATEGIC MARKETING EXECUTIVE: Technology-Driven Organizations

Global Marketing Strategies · Brand & Product Management · Market-Focused Product Development

Catalyst for profitable growth: Strategic, analytical, customer- and solution-focused marketing executive with proven success delivering strong results in sales growth, profitability, and account penetration:

- **134%** revenue growth over 5 years
- **40%** to **70%** market share for every product in digital testing equipment portfolio
- **42%** gross-margin improvement in the most challenging technology market in recent history
- **#1** revenue-generating product for 135-year-old company

Expertise in all aspects of marketing and sales strategies, planning, and execution for technology-based organizations. Exceptional track record of building high-performance teams and developing strong relationships and alliances with customers and channel partners. Equal success in launching marketing initiatives for new product introductions and product-line revitalization. Exceptional presentation skills.

EXPERIENCE AND ACHIEVEMENTS

Xaltex TECHNOLOGIES ($700M global test and measurement company)   New York , NY, 2003–Present

BUSINESS MANAGER / NEW BUSINESS PRODUCT MANAGER

Delivered 42% profit increase during challenging market conditions, driving product strategies and sales efficiencies across entire division. Hired to develop and implement sales and marketing programs to capitalize on new business opportunities. Concurrently, challenged to lead initiatives to improve performance of existing multimillion-dollar product line and resolve sales efficiency barriers.

- Developed new business model for innovative technology to generate **$20M** incremental business in 3 years—**$100K** revenue and **$1M+** sales funnel in first 3 months.
- Led a cross-functional rapid-action team in developing and implementing a web-based configuration/ quote tool for the global sales team that reduced customer quote times from **3** days to **15** minutes.
- Spearheaded product-line optimization that delivered exceptional profit performance during severe industry downturn:

	2002	2003	2004	2005
Revenue	$6.5M	$5M	$5M	$5.5M
Gross Margin	28%	60%	70%	70%

GREAT TREES COMPANY ($120M worldwide water analysis test equipment company)
Cincinnati, OH, 1998–2003

■ **PRODUCT MANAGER**

Transformed business from R&D- to market-driven, reversing declining sales and generating 134% growth in 5 years. Managed product line P&L and led combined marketing/engineering team. Analyzed markets; conceived long-range and competitive strategies; prepared marketing plans, budgets, and sales forecasts; initiated product improvements to meet changing market needs. Established program metrics and consistently held post-program evaluations to identify and institutionalize best practices.

- Delivered steady and substantial revenue growth:

	1997	1998	1999	2000	2001 (proj.)
Revenue	**$7.9M**	**$8.8M**	**$11.2M**	**$13.5M**	**$18.5M**
Growth	**-6%**	**+11%**	**+22%**	**+20%**	**+37%**

- Launched **12** successful new products in 4 years including 2 products introduced in the Americas through acquisition and successful integration of a European firm.
- Seized leading market share (**40%–70%**) for all products in my team's portfolio.
- Increased profits **15%** through marketing strategies that clearly articulated customer value to
- command premium pricing.
- Reestablished Great Rivers as the world leader in analytical testing, working collaboratively with sales, key customers, and EPA to produce a "disruptive technology" that overwhelmed the competition.
- Guided engineers out to the customer, leading to the design of high-profit, value-added products.
- Created a high-performance team. Defined vision, empowered team members to act, and led by example.

WROGHT SYSTEMS, INC.   Dallas, 1991–1997
(Privately held company, a leader in design of control systems for power generation applications)

■ **PROGRAM MANAGER,** 1995–1997

Accelerated product development and tightened cost/scheduling controls by formalizing project management practices division-wide. Promoted to full program management for industrial controls; managed cross-functional project teams in system design, development, and deployment.

- Cut new product introduction cycle times **50%** by implementing a formal project management system.
- Efficiently managed scope, schedule, and budget of multiple projects, resolving technical and business issues with internal and external customers.

■ **PRODUCT MARKETING MANAGER,** 1993–1995

Championed new business/product opportunity that set a company record for revenue generation. Provided leadership and direction to an international OEM sales team. Performed market research and developed strategic plans to increase sales, meet profit objectives, and penetrate new markets/accounts. Developed strong customer relationships that led to business opportunities.

- Initiated and closed 5-year contract to supply control systems for a large European power generation company; displaced competitor as vendor of choice. Assumed role of product champion and account manager, repeatedly removing internal barriers and renewing executive support for the project.
  - Generated **$20M** incremental revenue in 3 years and **$100M+** in 10 years
  - Product became the company's **#1** revenue generator for industrial power generation products.

- **ACCOUNT MANAGER / APPLICATION ENGINEER,** 1991–1993

Grew revenue 58% in 2 years, managing national OEM accounts and actively pursuing new business.

- Increased sales **30%** first year, **21%** second year; consistently exceeded divisional goals.
- Tapped to develop sales training seminars for US and international sales force.

EDUCATION

MS Technology Management   Wright State University, Dayton, OH
BS Computer Engineering / Minor—Mathematics   University of Cincinnati, Cincinnati, OH

Extensive professional development in marketing, management, product management, negotiation, sales.

AFFILIATIONS

Member American Management Association (AMA)
Member American Society for Testing and Materials (ASTM)
Former Member Board of Directors, Electrical Generation Systems Association (EGSA)

Marketing Leadership Initiatives: Smyxe Associates

■ **Revitalized branding and communications.**

Communications programs were outdated, content-deficient, and failed to communicate firm's value proposition or differentiators. Brand was unclear and visual identity chaotic.

Created project objectives: *simplicity—clarity—identity—image*. Built internal coalition of support and launched a comprehensive overhaul beginning with interviews with key stakeholders.

Implemented new promise line and directed redesign of entire visual identity. Led road show to introduce new identity in all 15 offices. Accelerated timetable to 7 months to coincide with 30th anniversary celebration.

Bottom Line:

- New website awarded "National Top 5" ranking for regional firms by Professional Services Monitor.
- Newsletter became a powerful lead generator, averaging 5 leads per issue on featured services.
- Tag line became litmus test for communications, proposals, client reports, staff evaluations, and hiring profiles.
- New image helped facilitate merger that resulted in successful expansion into New Jersey and the addition of critical expertise and leadership resources.
- Firm was positioned as a major regional force on par with national employers in its industry, attracting both experienced recruits and new college grads.

■ **Ignited business development.**

Growth had stalled in mature markets and awareness was low in regions targeted for expansion. Business development was unfocused and partners/managers (primary drivers of new business) lacked confidence in consultative selling.

Designed strategy to improve lead development and consultative selling skills of partners and managers. Set aggressive goal to earn 100% ROI on campaign cost within 12 months.

Bottom Line:

- Produced more than $60K in ongoing new annuity and project revenue in just 3 months, realizing a 300% ROI.
- Added 150 new self-identified "interested" prospects to database in a single test market.
- Program won the top national award from the Association of Accounting Marketing.

■ **Drove successful customer relationship management (CRM) initiative.**

Information systems for the firm's most valuable assets (clients, prospects, referral sources, alumni, staff capabilities and experience) were outdated, fragmented, unreliable, and unconnected to the financial system. There was no ability to track a client's total value to the firm or identify cross-sell opportunities.

The impact was wasted money, poor response times, duplication of efforts, and missed opportunities.

Initiated, developed, and sold partners on a major $350K CRM initiative (software, hardware, implementation, training, and ongoing database management). Established project goals and benchmarks. Created internal champions by recruiting an Advisory Committee of influential partners and staff. Selected vendors. Recruited and coached project manager and cross-functional project team.

Bottom Line:

- Captured immediate savings of $15K on production and mailing costs; return rate dropped from 10% to less than 2%.
- Enhanced reputation as trusted source of timely knowledge to clients.
- Gained ability to evaluate profitability by client, line of business, service, and geography, creating benchmarks for marketing performance and targets for growth.

ENGINEERING EXECUTIVE

Product R&D · Continuous Process Improvement & Cost Reduction · Lean Methodologies · Value Engineering Programs

Top performer in engineering leadership roles, delivering operational excellence and sustainable performance improvements through innovation, technology, and best-in-class manufacturing methodologies. Partner with business units and manufacturing operations to execute strategic business initiatives; able to translate customer/market needs to product solutions and establish market differentiation through technology, innovation, and patented products/processes.

Dedicated to utilizing all resources, including technology, to streamline processes, improve product quality, and drive revenue growth. Energized by "impossible" challenges. BSME, MBA.

Executive Endorsements: *"I really believe the life blood of a company is new product development, and there is absolutely no doubt… in my mind that you… are developing new and exciting products which will take [the company] to new heights."*—CEO, Dawlon-Kruz Industries

"Your dedication to innovation, to productivity, and to quality is exemplified in many of the 'extra' things you achieve or the way in which you achieve them."—VP Engineering, DK Engineered Products

EXPERIENCE AND ACHIEVEMENTS

KL ENGINEERED PRODUCTS, Lynchburg, VA   *#1 in its industry in the US; $600M subsidiary of Dawlon – Krut Industries, a Fortune 500 company*

■ **Engineering Director for New Business Development,** 2005–Present

Chosen to spearhead new business initiative, leveraging existing technologies and capabilities to meet strategic corporate goals of revenue growth and market-share expansion. Senior executive for the initiative. Develop strategic plan and lead an engineering team in implementing new products into production lines, streamlining and simplifying processes for rapid ramp-up, and providing engineering support to the marketing and sales team.

- Outperformed first-year revenue goal—currently on pace to deliver $7M revenue, 75% above target.
- Jump-started new initiative by personally landing first 2 contracts, generating $500K seed capital.
- Accelerated product launch through a modular approach that reduces engineering procedures. Brought 40 new
- products online in one year, 4X–5X more than company average.
- Developed a returnable packaging system for small components; delivered 25% cost savings to the customer.
- Evaluated a $3.5M tooling acquisition, prepared cost justification, recommended go-ahead, and modified acquired tooling into existing production systems. Delivered $15MM revenue—more than 3X ROI—in first year.

- **Director of Research & Development,** 2001–2005

  In newly created internal consulting/R&D leadership role, led numerous initiatives across all of the company's business groups to improve manufacturing processes, materials, and results. Managed 2 R&D engineers, 1 group manager, and 15 engineering services staff; consulted to the company's Metal, Wood, and Plastics product groups.

  Analyzed all areas of plant operations and R&D initiatives, identifying product, waste-reduction, and cost-control opportunities. Devised and executed 3-year prioritized action plan to achieve strategic objectives.

  - Delivered millions of dollars in cost reductions—e.g., cut 30% from component manufacturing by eliminating non-value added processes.
  - Drove innovative product development to generate profitable new revenue:
    - Generated $15MM first-year sales in a new market via a new line constructed from composite materials.
    - Invigorated stagnant product line, added 12 new products, and increased profitability 30%.
    - Conceived new feature for industrial markets, delivering $250K incremental annual revenue.

- **Corporate Director of Engineering and Product Development,** 1998–2001

  Improved manufacturing performance by implementing Lean methodologies and continuous improvement initiatives. Directed all engineering projects in 5 U.S. and 2 international plants (Mexico and Canada). Managed $2.5MM engineering budget, $10MM capital budget, and 27 engineering and management staff.

  - Achieved $2MM annual savings through an aggressive Continuous Cost Improvement Program.
  - Implemented 3P (Production Preparation Process) and led numerous Kaizen and 3P events in all plants.
  - Conceived and launched a 3-tier talent-development plan: high school mentorship, college co-op, and the elite Engineering/Management Development Program, a 2-year business-wide rotational assignment combined with an intensive MBA-like program (developed complete curriculum).
    - Transformed company image to the point where the EMDP program has a waiting list at top colleges.
    - Achieved 100% success/retention rate in 5+ years; earned President's Award.

- **Engineering Manager/Model Shop Manager,** 1991–1998

  Reduced the cycle times of virtually every activity, managing all model work for the company's 3 product divisions as well as all engineering projects in the Metal Group. Supervised 9 staff.

  - Identified profitable product innovation; developed prototype and successfully market-tested idea for composite designs that could be produced 30% below cost of existing materials.
  - Developed and implemented several new product designs and features, earning numerous patents and helping company to retain its position as a market leader and innovator.

- **Senior Engineer, Special Projects,** 1985–1991

Led numerous initiatives—both cost/process improvements and major capital projects—for all areas of production. Prepared feasibility studies for new production lines; purchased millions of dollars in tooling and equipment; set up new manufacturing facilities; designed and implemented new processes. Project highlights include:

- Coordinated $1.75MM renovation of engineering R&D center.
- Saved $150K through an interplant hardware packaging program (Kanban) to eliminate corrugated boxes.
- Curbed losses from inefficient plant heating, resulting in $75K cost savings.
- Brought custom production shop online under budget in 90 days. Designed flexible tooling and features to accommodate product variances and volume growth—today shop represents $5MM incremental revenue.

EARLY CAREER

Manufacturing/Tooling Engineer, KENYON MEDICAL SYSTEMS, 1982–1986: Evaluated and purchased new technology capital equipment; coordinated vendor tooling purchases for new product manufacturing requirements; managed 5 tool room staff. Served as plant Safety Director.

- Led numerous technology, tooling, and production cost-savings and improvement programs.
  - Parts redesign: $450K savings.
  - New fixture and tool supply control system: $160K savings, lead time reductions for both standard products (60%) and custom items (70%).
  - Maintenance program for wire termination: $60K cost reduction.

PROFESSIONAL PROFILE

Education	**MBA,** Randolph-Macon College, Lynchburg, VA, 1989 **BS Mechanical Engineering,** University of Virginia, Charlottesville, VA, 1979 **Advanced Management Continuous Improvement Program / Toyota Production System,** 1992 **Shingijutsu Kaizen Training,** Japan, 1993, 1998, and 1999
Patents	Awarded 24 US patents (additional 3 pending) for product innovations; more than 50% of patents converted to revenue-producing products.
Affiliation	Senior Member, Society of Manufacturing Engineers
Languages	Fluent speaking and writing Italian; conversational Spanish and French.

Entrepreneurial and growth-focused executive, twice building regional services businesses to millions of dollars in revenue and market leadership.

- **Top performance** in Sears partnership, growing the relationship to #1 in service and #2 in national sales volume among 370 contractors across the country.
- **Proven skills** as a team builder and motivational leader able to inspire staff to excellence.
- **Hands-on management experience** in all facets of the business, with notable contributions as a sales leader and finance manager, able to build lean organizations and capture emerging business opportunities.
- **Service orientation** and ability to make integrity and customer service prime differentiators in the market.

EXPERIENCE AND ACHIEVEMENTS

LA BRINY MECHANICAL SERVICES, INC.   Encinitas, CA, 2000–Present

■ **President**

Launched full-service repair and installation company, growing into a major service arm of Sears retail organizations in 3 U.S. regions. Defined vision/strategy emphasizing integrity and service as competitive differentiators. Grew the business from start-up to $6MM revenue, 38 staff, in 5 years.

In 2005, recruited a new, highly talented executive team (CEO, CFO, CIO) to ignite massive growth (to $200MM by 2007) and position the company for spin-off.

- **Growth:** Built a strongly ethical business foundation with exceptional pricing, quality, and workmanship; achieved lean operations through ROI-focused expense control; and delivered steady revenue growth:

	2001	2002	2003	2004	2005	2006 (proj.)
Revenue	$1.6MM	$2.1MM	$2.5MM	$4.4MM	$6MM	$25MM

- **Strategic business:** Became a prominent and valued Sears partner:
  - #2 in sales volume among 370 nationwide
  - #1 in quality service rating
  - Top 10% in attach rate—driven through partnering and relationship-building with store staff and managers

- **Expansion:** At the request of Sears executives, took over new regions nationally to improve sales, service, and the Sears brand value in those markets:
  - Washington State, June 2005
  - Phoenix, October 2005

- **Service orientation:**
  - Personally requested to provide intensive customer-service training to Sears' West Coast call center.
  - Introduced compensation plan innovative for the industry, paying service technicians salary rather than commission to drive customer-first philosophy.

O'MALLEY INSTALLATION SERVICES   Encinitas, CA, 1984–2000

- **President,** 1992–2000

  Assumed ownership of the business, inheriting steep financial challenges and driving a turnaround to more than triple revenues.

  - **Growth:** Increased revenues from $1.6MM in 1984 to $5MM in 2000.
  - **Diversification:** Launched home-improvement subsidiary and grew to $2.7MM gross revenue in 3 years.
  - **Strategic business:** Managed and grew Sears business from start-up to $2MM annual revenues.

- **Additional Roles & Performance Highlights,** 1984–1992

  Learned the business from the ground up, advancing to new areas of responsibility to gain expertise and tackle significant business challenges.

  - **Finance Manager:** Identified accounting discrepancies and assumed responsibility for the company's financial operations—A/R, A/P, payroll, worker's comp, liability, and vehicle maintenance as well as oversight of 8 administrative staff and 30 field technicians.
    - Overhauled processes, upgraded technology, and eliminated source of significant financial loss.
    - Developed proprietary system for tracking daily cash flow to the penny.

  - **Operations Manager:** Oversaw field service and fleet of company-owned vehicles. Continuously sought opportunities to cut costs, improve efficiency, and increase service.
    - Saved $60K annually by redesigning service flow and assigning dedicated truck/driver for appliance pick-ups.

  - **Sales Manager:** Developed new business and managed major accounts including regional appliance dealers, Lowe's, Sears, and Home Depot.
    - Recognized market opportunity with the arrival of Lowe's in the San Diego market; cold-called to develop first Lowe's business and grew to the company's #1 account.

Active volunteer in the San Diego community.
References provided upon request.

JOHN CITIZEN   **SENIOR FINANCE AND OPERATIONS**   CONTACT DETAILS

■ **SENIOR FINANCE & OPERATIONS EXECUTIVE**

Global Operations · Revenue & Profit Performance · Business Analysis · M&A Deal Structuring

Track record of integrity, leadership, and results, driving the attainment of business, revenue, expense, and profit targets for Fujitsu global operations and leading an innovative start-up in the Americas. Expert in identifying strategic business opportunities, analyzing value and impact across complex enterprises, and orchestrating implementation, acquisition, divestiture, or other transaction.

Accomplished team builder, business partner, and negotiator who never fails to win consensus. Effective leader of multicultural teams in diverse locales worldwide; fluent in English, Japanese, and French.

EXPERIENCE HIGHLIGHTS

- Created start-up company for the sales and distribution of medical equipment; earned elite certification as business partner of GE Medical Systems.
- As CFO of $3B services segment for Fujitsu, led multinational team in delivering 109% of profit goal.
- Identified, analyzed, and executed $200M in M&A transactions for Fujitsu Corporate HQ.
- Achieved 21% cost reductions as Controller of $800M in Fujitsu internal IT investments.
- Established a regional Finance & Administration function in 5 countries.

EXPERIENCE AND ACHIEVEMENTS

MEDI-DISTRIBUTIONS   Norwalk, CT

■ **FOUNDER / GENERAL MANAGER**   2004–2006

Led start-up firm from concept to strategic partnerships and revenue generation. Identified business opportunity in the competitive North/Central American healthcare market. Created business plan; negotiated lines of credit; established supplier and technical support relationships with Canadian manufacturer of a new brand of medical endoscopes. Led rapid launch and managed all marketing, sales, finance, and business operations.

- Secured critical marketing/business relationship as a certified business partner of GE Medical Systems.
- Generated revenue within 3 months of launch through aggressive business-building with distributors, hospitals, and clinics in Canada, Mexico, and Costa Rica.
- Earned product trial with one of the largest medical procurement companies in Central America.

FUJITSU   Asia, Europe, US

■ **CFO INTEGRATED TECHNOLOGY SERVICES, Fujitsu Europe**   2003–2004

Ensured profitable performance of $3B revenue business. Established quarterly and yearly targets for the 5 regions making up Fujitsu's European business; approved investment business cases and tracked performance toward defined goals. Managed multicultural team of 15 dispersed at international locations.

Provided functional guidance to 5 regional CFOs and built strong collaborative relationships to ensure revenue and profit attainment.

- Nimbly managed moving targets—constantly revised upward throughout the year—and protected the most profitable business in the portfolio to achieve excellent year-end results:
  - 109% of revised profit goal
  - 93% of revised revenue target, 101% of initial target
- Developed road maps for revenue protection and expense reductions to secure the bottom line.

■ DIRECTOR FINANCIAL OFFERINGS, Fujitsu Europe   2002–2003

Delivered profitability nearly 1.5X target as senior negotiator/final authority on all major contracts for a major global account. Reviewed all proposals prior to submission to the customer and directly negotiated terms and pricing on key contracts with the client's senior executives. Worked closely with administrative team that had direct responsibility for the global customer relationship.

- Achieved 105% of annual revenue target and 145% of profit goal.
- Made and kept promise to turn around all proposals within 24 hours—regardless of time zone differences from the Far East to Europe and the Americas. Built reputation for reliability and integrity in all regions worldwide.

■ BUSINESS DEVELOPMENT/M&A CONSULTANT, Fujitsu North America, New York, NY   1999–2002

Identified, evaluated, and recommended major investments of strategic value to Fujitsu— mergers, acquisitions, and divestitures. Worked in conjunction with major New York investment bankers and business law firms to identify and assess potential transactions; performed business and financial evaluations; submitted deal structure to Fujitsu senior management for approval; shepherded transactions to closure.

- Closed $200M in transactions in 18 months.
- Pulled together diverse functional teams for each project and led through complex analysis and structured decision-making. Established expectations and firmly adhered to original project timelines.
- Also served as Fujitsu corporate M&A contact for Latin American countries.

■ CORPORATE FINANCE ANALYST, Fujitsu Japan, Tokyo, Japan   1996–1999

Developed business and financial targets for $16B division, building strong links and constructive dialogue flow with division CFO and Finance team. Prepared and presented financial review sessions and performance evaluations to executive team. Created action plans for expense reduction to boost profitability.

- Using a "no surprises" approach, carefully managed information flow between division and corporate HQ, resulting in consistently excellent working relationships.
- Earned 100% approval rate on all investment business cases reviewed/recommended to Fujitsu CFO.

■ **CONTROLLER, Internal IT Investments, Fujitsu, New York, NY**   1994–1996

Outperformed aggressive cost-cutting goal, reporting to newly created position of CIO in the US and leading initiatives to better manage and control the company's IT investments in North America.

- Strategically focused efforts on projects that made up 80% of total internal IT expense. Interviewed, questioned, and challenged project owners, funding entities, and end users; created a prioritized list of projects for divestiture or closure. Gained executive approval and drove implementation.
- Achieved 21% cost reduction in 2 years vs. 15% target.

■ **EARLY CAREER WITH FUJITSU:** Fast-track advancement through increasingly responsible financial and management positions in Asia, Europe, and the US.

- Executive Assistant, Europe General Manager of Marketing & Services, Paris, France
- Manager, Performance & Outlook Assessment, Europe, Paris, France
- Program Manager, North American Manufacturing Plans & Controls, Chicago, IL
- Financial Operations Manager, U.K., London, England
- Finance & Administration Manager, Singapore
- Billing Manager, Singapore
- Associate Financial Analyst, Corporate HQ, Tokyo, Japan
- Accounting Analyst, Corporate HQ, Tokyo, Japan

EDUCATION

BS Economics, 1979 University of Michigan
MBA, 1998, Harvard Business School

Fujitsu Executive Education Highlights

- Acquisition Seminar, 1999
- Senior Management Course, 1995
- Advanced Management School, 1990
- Financial Management, Senior Financial Management, Accounting Management, 1978–1983

Dual US/Japanese Citizenship

HUMAN RESOURCES EXECUTIVE

EXAMPLES OF EFFECTIVENESS

- **Launching a New Training Function for a Start-up Division** *(SAI GLOBAL)*

  Driving force behind strategy, planning, and launch of training organization for a new division; transformed initial vision of "training programs" into a strategically focused training curriculum closely aligned with organizational mission and goals. Gained executive buy-in for new strategy through advocacy, education, and persuasiveness.

- **Guiding Emerging Leaders in Leading-Edge Human Performance Methodologies** *(U.S. Air Force/Consultant)*

  Introduced team of inexperienced performance analysts to the latest methodologies in human performance consulting as well as strategies to establish themselves as a trusted resource to their internal customers.

- **Reducing Costs through Streamlining and Training** *(Ernst & Young)*

  Developed and managed training and performance improvement project. Consulted with Accounting/ Finance Manager to reduce department expenses. Analyzed department's workflow, streamlined operations, and created a cross-functional on-the-job training program. Saved $115,000 in expenses while maintaining department production and efficiency levels.

- **Leading Process to Reduce Bad Debt** *(Ernst & Young)*

  Initiated and led effort of Quality Improvement Team to support Regional Controller's debt-reduction business goal. Audited existing consumer collection process, recommended and implemented cross-organizational changes. Produced the largest bad-debt reduction in the company's history, saving $1 million.

- **Reducing Risk of Litigation** *(American Financial Group)*

  Led team in developing an employment law curriculum. Addressed company legal liabilities during rapid expansion, which included the hiring of 1200 new managers. Curriculum adopted by international business units.

- **Heading Company Effort to Establish Industry Leadership** *(American Financial Group)*

  Initiated and led education design team to develop and implement an evaluation strategy, which included best practice standards and competencies. Resulted in the identification of process improvements, an employee competency development process, a method for linking design materials to business objectives, and a means to ensure that client training met or exceeded industry best practice standards.

- **Developing Innovative Partnership to Benefit Front-Line Management** *(Ernst & Young)*

Managed training curriculum, vendor, and budget for a regional facility of 1200. Consulted with executives to initiate Leadership Development Training. Developed beneficial partnership with state university, gaining added expertise and saving $52,000 (25% total training expenditures) by tapping into state grant training funds.

- **Managing Transition to Smoke-Free Workplace** *(Ernst & Young)*

Involved smokers and non-smokers in selecting a smoking-cessation training vendor and developing employee communication and facilities modification plans. Partnership with employees across all levels of the organization produced a smooth transition without employee complaints.

CAREER HISTORY

Executive HR Consultant (Clients include U.S. Air Force, Cinergy)	2005–Present
Training Manager	Sai Global, 2004–2005
HR Senior Consultant	American Financial Group, 1999–2004
Human Resources Administrator	Ernst & Young, 1996–1998
Progressive HR and Management Roles	Ernst & Young, 1988–1996

SENIOR EXECUTIVE: Technology • Operations • Business Process Transformation • Global Enterprises

Strategist, change leader, and driving force behind technology advances and business improvements that support corporate objectives.

Versatile executive with a career-long record of innovation and results, leading technology and operations for national and global enterprises with challenging computing, communications, and information processing needs. Expert in aligning technology strategies with corporate goals and driving major initiatives through dispersed and complex enterprises. Broad range of complementary strengths, from vision/strategy and tactical execution through communication/presentation and ability to gain support for major change initiatives.

Reliably delivered cost savings, efficiency improvements, cycle-time reductions, and profitability enhancements through leading-edge methodologies including Six Sigma and Crosby. Expanded role to include business development, corporate communications, and involvement in all key business initiatives. Valued member of the senior business leadership team. MBA.

EXPERIENCE AND ACHIEVEMENTS

Avery Smith Insurance Services, Inc.   **Greenville, SC, 2000–Present**
$500MM TPC administrator for workers' compensation, liability, and property insurance.

VICE PRESIDENT INFORMATION SERVICES

Drove total transformation of Information Services from outdated, inefficient organization to state-of-the-art business partner supporting company growth in all areas. Crossed all areas of the company to contribute to strategic, business-wide initiatives outside the realm of IS. Recognized for outstanding achievement with rare honor of the company's Innovator Award (awarded just once in the last 5 years).

- **Technology Improvements**
  - Led a vigorous 18-month turnaround. More than doubled size of staff (currently 100), added new quality assurance capability, revolutionized underlying technologies supporting the business, and led a company- wide change management initiative to gain widespread support for new technologies.
  - Led ongoing projects to automate processes and transform highly paper-intensive business to electronic data management. Added capabilities to improve productivity and performance at every desktop in the company.
  - Introduced rigorous project management methodologies and reengineered IS systems, processes, and workflows for maximum productivity.
  - Key member of IT team that evaluated and ensured 100% compliance with Sarbanes-Oxley requirements.

- **Strategic Initiatives**
  - Launched first-in-the-industry web portal allowing clients instant access to account activity and the claims management process. Serves 15,000 clients and attracts more than 15 million visits per month.
  - Initiated e-commerce capabilities, integrated with vendor systems for efficiency and tight control of contracts/performance.

- Drove outsourcing initiative, identifying the right processes to outsource and selecting/implementing an offshore partner. Improved accuracy of highly detailed processes while achieving $2M+ annual cost savings.
- As evangelist for new initiatives, commenced company-wide communications program, regularly visiting field offices and presenting at key sales and marketing meetings to connect business operations with technology changes and strategic plans.

■ Business Development
- Instrumental in generating $80M in new revenue, as a core member of strategic business development team.
- Delivering sales presentations to key accounts, communicated technology capabilities as a competitive advantage.
- Represented the company at trade shows, learning customer needs and relating them to company strengths and technology capabilities.
- Built recognition through published articles and keynote presentations that position the company as an industry leader.

Auto Auctions, Inc.
Greenville, SC, 1998–2000
$100M company, pioneering online site for auctioning repossessed vehicles.

DIRECTOR, INFORMATION SERVICES

Launched Internet presence, a key component of the business strategy, and strengthened technology infrastructure to support robust growth with advanced capabilities and operational efficiencies.

■ Performance Highlights
- Directed development of corporate intranet and Internet website with fully enabled e-commerce capability supporting 600,000 hits per week.
- Overhauled the computing infrastructure to include mainstream operating systems, software development tools, and database components.
- Increased development productivity 30% by implementing standard quality-assurance programs, application- design architectures, and project-management methodologies.
- Consolidated data and order management from 40 remote auction facilities into a single common data center, producing $2M annual savings and ensuring efficient, reliable, 24x7 system availability.
- Expanded technology services to key customers, implementing digital imaging, EDI/EFT, and custom client/server vehicle-management systems to enable attainment of $80M in new sales contracts.

Mining Equipment Corporation
Birmingham, AL, 1990–1998
A global market leader in agricultural and construction equipment.

Repeatedly asked to take on new challenges in diverse areas of the company—both US and international. Planned and developed or evaluated/purchased systems and technology to support complex business, financial, and communications needs of the worldwide enterprise.

MANAGER, PRODUCT MANAGEMENT SYSTEMS (1998–1998)
MANAGER, PRODUCT DISTRIBUTION SYSTEMS (1995–1996)
MANAGER, FINANCIAL SYSTEMS (1993–1995)
MANAGER, INTERNATIONAL SYSTEMS (1991–1993)
PROJECT MANAGER, CORPORATE SYSTEMS GROUP (1990–1991)

- ■ **Performance Highlights**
  - Created 5-year strategic technology plan and gained executive support for recommended investments, including financial and order-management systems for the global enterprise; delivered more than $15M annual savings.
  - Managed company financial systems activities in support of $350M company IPO.
  - Led development and implementation of automated business process system to manage sale of $3.7B equipment financing portfolio; reduced annual interest expense by 61%.
  - Worked extensively in Asian, Pacific Rim, and Australian sales regions and subsidiaries, implementing infrastructure upgrades and new technologies and services. Managed 15 staff in Singapore data center.

Esso Corporation   **Fairfax, VA, 1983–1990**

Competed through rigorous selection process to earn entry to year-long management training program covering all areas of process refining. Advanced steadily to new challenges in Engineering, Marketing, Finance, and Information Technology.

SENIOR SYSTEMS ANALYST, US SUPPLY DIVISION (1989–1990)
SENIOR FINANCIAL ANALYST (1987–1989)
GROUP LEAD, FINANCE (1986–1987)
LOSS PREVENTION ENGINEER (1984–1986)
MANAGEMENT TRAINING PROGRAM (1983–1984)

EDUCATION AND PROFESSIONAL DEVELOPMENT

MBA, Finance   **Georgetown University, Washington, DC, 1986**
BS, Chemical Engineering   **Virginia Tech, Blacksburg, VA, 1983**
Six Sigma and Crosby Quality Training

Bibliography and Useful Webpages

Bonnie Kurka, Career Daze – Blogspot – (2006) – Values and Career Choices, Tulsa, Oklahoma, United States

Time Thoughts – Goal Setting: http://www.timethoughts.com/goal-setting.htm

HandBook Entry - Science – Monash University Education – Undergraduates - Employments objectives

Career OWL Resources – Resumes – Objectives: www.CareerOwl.ca

Get Interviews http://www.salary.com/series/get-interviews/

Business – Love to Know – Resume Objectives:
http://business.lovetoknow.com/wiki/Resume_Objective_Examples

Articles on Jobs – entertainment – Engineers – Business – Professional blogs –
http://jobs.entertainmentengineering.com/

Get elected to the career of your dreams :
http://www.beyond.com/articles/get-elected-to-the-career-of-your-dreams-lessons-3997-article.html

Lessons learned from the candidates:
http://learning.blogs.nytimes.com/2012/08/28/2012-election-unit-who-are-the-candidates/

Find articles.com : http://www.search.com/search

LCC Education – Employment – Alumni – Setting career goals

Solve Your problems – setting goals – setting career goals : Chapter Four, Houghton Mifflin Company

Career Playbook – Guide to Interview Questions:
http://www.careerplaybook.com/guide/interview_questions.asp

Resume Examples

http://www.cyberneur.com/

Your Best Impression – Resumes: http://www.yourbestimpression.com/

Advance Yourself : http://www.advance-yourself.com.au/

Tom Hannemann, Article: How resumes optimise interview time

EPR – Career Change - http://www.epr.com.au/

Blue Sky Resumes: http://blueskyresumes.com/

Dorothy Leeds, article, Get the Job you want –

Tom Jaz, Lowell Hellervik, David C.Gilmore : Behavior Description Interviewing, Prentice Hall, Inc. 1986 pg 3 -41

Job Hunt

Liz Ryan, article, Job Search Networking –

Weddles's newsletters: http://www.weddles.com/newsletters.htm

The Economist

About the Author

Edua Potor lived in several countries in Europe and Central Africa, prior to choosing Australia as her home base.

She started her career in Executive Recruitment in 1987 and over the years interviewed well over 13,000 executive candidates, working with 120 of the top 500 National and International Companies.

Her experience includes running her own company prior to selling into a multi-disciplinary recruitment firm, where she took on the role of General Manager and Human Resources Manager.

Her investigative mind, industry experience and understanding of the importance of finding the executive talent that "makes a difference", saw a career re-alignment with her expansion into research and search for Executive Leaders.

Edua has a passion for Science, a degree in Homeopathic Medicine and is the founder of the "Ageless Executive", offering successful strategies to rejuvenate your body and your mind and to champion the executive spirit

Her post graduate training and continuing education includes anti-ageing medicine, super-nutrition and longevity.

Her life long spiritual journey has led her to travel to many countries inspiring her to support shifts in perceptions in others, leading to the natural state of awakening.

She is an enthusiastic student of life aspiring to the marriage of health, science and spirit.